MONSTERS IN THE WOODS

TIM HAUSERMAN

MONSTERS IN THE WOODS

BACKPACKING WITH CHILDREN

University of Nevada Press
Reno & Las Vegas

University of Nevada Press, Reno, Nevada 89557 USA
Copyright © 2007 by University of Nevada Press
Photographs copyright © 2007 by Tim Hauserman, unless otherwise noted
All rights reserved
Manufactured in the United States of America
Design by Kaelin Chappell Broaddus

Library of Congress Cataloging-in-Publication Data
Hauserman, Tim, 1958–
Monsters in the woods : backpacking with children / Tim Hauserman.
p. cm.
Includes bibliographical references and index.
ISBN 978-0-87417-711-4 (pbk. : alk. paper)
1. Backpacking. 2. Hiking for children. 3. Camping. I. Title.
GV199.6.H38 2007
796.51083—DC22
2006037615

The paper used in this book is made from 30 percent post-consumer
waste materials and meets the requirements of American
National Standard for Information Sciences—Permanence of Paper
for Printed Library Materials, ANSI Z.48–1984. Binding
materials were selected for strength and durability.
First Printing
16   15   14   13   12   11   10   09   08   07   5   4   3   2   1
Frontispiece: Two girls above the lake. Photograph by Tim Hauserman

To Hannah and Sarah:
Thanks for the quiet moonlit nights,
the smooth granite rocks,
the gentle ripples across the cold lake,
and the warmth of your laughter and love.

CONTENTS

ILLUSTRATIONS

PREFACE

This book is a guide to backpacking with children. It is intended for experienced backpackers as well as newcomers. I have tried to provide you with all of the information you will need to backpack with your children, and none of the information that you don't need. In addition, while the book is geared toward backpacking with children, you should find everything you need to hit the trail without children as well. This book has purposely been kept light enough that you can take it with you on the trip (if you feel it is too heavy to carry, sneak it into your kid's pack when he's not looking. Don't worry; it will make him tough).

There are officially at least 2 million different methods of backpacking. Lots of people will read this book and say, "Well, that can't be right, I was taught to do it this way." Or "No, they should do it this way, they shouldn't take this, they should take that, blah, blah, blah." While there are certainly lots of wrong ways to backpack, there is no absolutely right way to head out into the wilderness. My method is what I have learned in Tim's Backpacking School of Hard Knocks. At this school, I was forced to read a lot of books, talk to a lot of experienced backpackers, and do a lot of homework. The good part was that my homework was to put on my backpack and head into the mountains with my children, with my friends, and by myself.

If you are a beginning backpacker I hope you learn a lot from this book, but don't stop here. Read lots of other books, go hiking, and start your own School of Hard Knocks. If you are an experienced backpacker, I am sure that you could teach me a lot, but hopefully you can learn a few things from this book as well.

A few words before we begin . . . Any outdoor activity has the potential to be dangerous. Any information provided to you in this book should not substitute for making your own decisions about where or when to hike and how to conduct yourself. You should decide for yourself whether you and everyone in your group are capable of handling any trip that you embark upon.

Also note that the described trails may have been abandoned or wiped out by floods or avalanches—check with local officials in the area you will be hiking to determine the latest travel conditions. Even a well-maintained trail can be dangerous during certain weather conditions; prepare accordingly.

The wilderness and the woods are wonderful places to be. You will learn about nature and yourself, but it's also important to be careful out there. You are responsible for your own actions. Become knowledgeable. Make smart decisions. Always prepare for the environment you will be entering. And have fun.

So sit down by a warm fire, grab a cup of hot chocolate, and begin to fantasize about cool mountain lakes, warm sunny meadows and the sound of children laughing.

MONSTERS IN THE WOODS

CHAPTER 1

Why, Who, When, Where?

I like to read, enjoy the scenery, spend quality time with my
dad, sit quietly and think to myself about life, go swimming,
play cards, go pee wherever I want, sleep in the afternoon,
drink hot cocoa, and more.
—Sarah Hauserman, 14

Why Backpack with Your Kids?

Perhaps you can only live life to the fullest when you are childlike.
The child in you comes out when you walk through the woods and
smell the trees, when you touch pine needles and flowers, or run
your hands over smooth rock. When you feel the cold, clear water
of a mountain lake numbing your toes. Gazing for an hour at the
stars or the first bright rays of morning sunshine. Hearing through
a child's ears the sweet, high singing of birds, or wind-driven water
lapping up against the rocky shoreline. We can escape the mun-
dane and be the happy carefree child within us, if we can just make
it into the wilderness. There we can sit and feel what is around us,
and find that inner child who has been hiding for much too long
inside our big grown-up bodies. The music of nature is the same
music that is in our hearts. We just need to go to nature to begin
the melody. While you can hear the melody when you are in the

Patty-caking at Dardanelles Lake.

wilderness as an adult, it can sound even sweeter when you spend a
night in the wilderness with your child.

At least in small-town America, a generation ago kids spent
every day playing outside. They understood nature because it was
part of their life. They were out fishing, or looking for frogs, or
just watching the clouds go by as they lazily threw rocks into the
lake. Now, our society has decided that it is not safe for kids to be
out in the woods doing "nothing." Instead they need to always be
busy. We have decided that children need to go right from school
to ballet, or soccer, or some other structured program. Then we
rush home so that they have time to do the piles of homework
dumped on them every night. I don't remember doing that much
homework when I was young, do you? But I do remember spending my summer throwing rocks into the lake, swimming all day, and
lying on sandy beaches for hours on end. In the winter we shifted
to snowball fights or playing football on the street. We were inside

only to eat and sleep, or when the parents were away and we could sneak in and watch TV. If our parents were around they wanted us outside and out of their hair, and we gladly obliged. Of course, if you wanted to spend a little more time inside, Mom was happy to give you lots of chores to do to keep you busy. That's OK Mom, we're happy to get out of here and play outside!

Now, even those of us who live in the mountains drag our children from one activity to the other before they hit the books around the woodstove. Even if they are doing structured outdoor programs like skiing or running, our children don't spend much time cooling their jets out in the woods. They certainly haven't spent hours just sitting with a toe in the water or watching the clouds go by. Of course, they are quite skilled at spending hours sitting in a chair and watching TV or playing video games (before staying up late to finish all that homework that they forgot to do).

The question isn't why backpack with your kids? The question is what took you so long? It is not that complicated. Spend an hour or two reading the rest of this book (and carrying out its suggestions), purchase or borrow a few things that you need, and you're ready to go.

To me, backpacking with my children is by far the best time I spend with them. It is one-on-one time without the distractions of civilization. Away from phones, TV, ballet practice, toys, and computers you can actually spend time talking about anything or everything, or most importantly, nothing, with your youngsters. While experiencing the beauty of nature, your children will learn important life lessons that no classroom can teach. As your kids get older (and try to be even older than they are), backpacking is a chance for them to play again. A time to be young children no matter what their age. To do simple tasks and focus on just the basics of life. They can learn that just like millions of people for millions of years before them, they really can get by without all the luxuries of civilization.

So I implore you to get your children to put down the basketball or the flute for a few days, turn the TV off, and walk out the door so they can learn a few important things:

How to set up a tent in five minutes or less when the rain is about to come down.

How to set up a tarp in 30 seconds or less when the rain and hail are coming down really hard.

How to occupy themselves for a few hours in a tent while the rain and hail come down outside.

How to go to the bathroom in the woods, without peeing on their pants.

How to fix a really good meal just by boiling some water. At least it will seem really good when they are in the middle of nowhere, and there are no other alternatives.

How to get along with friends or relatives when spending three days with them in camp (or worse yet, inside the cramped quarters of a small tent).

How to get a good night's sleep even when the ground is hard, and they are scared of bears.

How to get through the next day even if they didn't sleep the night before, because they thought they heard a bear.

How to love the day when they do nothing but swim, sit on warm rocks, and futz around camp.

How to love the outdoors and learn how to treat it with respect.

How to have a nice, quiet conversation with Mom or Dad.

Once you go through the work of getting organized and learning all the things you need to know and actually hit the trail, you will discover why you are doing this. When you have your tent set up and are lying next to your daughter listening only to the wind in the trees and the distant lapping of water against rocks, you will understand and be glad. Of course, when you are still lying there at 4 AM and listening to the creaking noise that you know must be a bear instead of sleeping you might have second thoughts. But wait until you see rays of sunshine hitting that granite face across the lake from your tent first thing in the morning. And then see the reflection of that mountain in the perfect stillness of the lake. You will be converted.

Who Gets to Go?

While both of my children like to backpack, or at least I think they do, it has worked the best for me to take one child at a time with a friend and that friend's dad. My tent holds two people as long as one is an adult and the other is a fairly narrow child. And you really don't want to carry a tent that holds three, because it will be quite a bit heavier. Bringing the friend is a good idea, because, although I am sure you are always riveting company, kids like to have a friend to play with. The friend's dad or mom comes along because you are not naive enough to carry all the supplies for two children and yourself, are you? If both of your children want to come along together, because they can't go a couple days without a really good fight, you have a bit of a sticky wicket unless you can convince a spouse or friend to come along. If both spouses or significant others are eager to go, a family of four can easily backpack together. Be forewarned that if you have four people you will most likely need two tents, four sleeping bags, four sleeping pads, and a lot of other stuff as well. The good news is that you will only need one stove and water filter.

For me, one-on-one time with just one child makes for a special occasion. There are no distractions, and you actually have a

Whatever you do, don't forget the jammies with the bears on them. Photo by Denese Pillsbury

rare opportunity to focus on your child. Some other parents can't imagine the whole family not coming along. Make your choice and plan accordingly. One factor in the decision may be the age of your children. Once children are old enough to carry their share of the load, it is much easier to take the whole family.

When Is the Right Age to Start Backpacking?

If you want your kids to be happily hiking along, carrying some of their own belongings, and being involved in the whole experience, then in general your child should be at least seven years old (with some exceptions, of course). If you and your spouse are desperate to go backpacking and are willing to take along a one-year-old baby, go ahead, but realize it will require a lot of extra work. Consider the joy of hiking around with dirty diapers in your backpack. Also, while one person gets to carry the little darling, the other is responsible for carrying the supplies for all three of you. You may want to make it a short trip or start out car camping. For more information on the special considerations for backpacking with infants or toddlers, refer to chapter 3.

In reality, while there are challenges at every age, almost any child can go backpacking. You just need to plan around the needs of your child and have some patience. OK, have lots of patience. Perhaps the story of Mary Chambers will put it all in perspective.

When she was seven years old, Mary hiked the entire Tahoe Rim Trail with her parents to become member number 61 of the Tahoe Rim Trail 165 Mile Club (those who have hiked the entire trail). It is no surprise that she became the club's youngest member. While this was quite an accomplishment, Mary was just getting warmed up. First, just for kicks, she hiked the TRT one more time in 2003. Then a year later, at the ripe old age of 10, she again set out with her parents and became the youngest person to backpack the entire Pacific Crest Trail from Mexico to Canada, all 2,650 miles of it. So how does a seven- or a ten-year-old find the wherewithal to tackle these incredible feats?

Mary's mother, Barbara Egbert, says one key is that the family does not have a television, and they have always dedicated themselves to spending time outdoors. They began hiking and backpacking when Mary was an infant. She would ride in Mom's baby pack, while Dad carried all the gear for the three of them. Later, when Mary began walking, sometimes she would walk and sometimes she would ride in the pack. While Mary's parents took it slow and easy, she fell in love with hiking and got stronger and stronger as the years went by. The Tahoe Rim Trail was their first major backpack trip, and, according to Barbara's description of it in the Tahoe Rim Trail Association's *Trail Blazer*, it sounds like Mom and

Dad had the toughest time of it, with major blisters on their feet. Not that it was a piece of cake for Mary. "We kept going, through bee stings, heat, dirt, and hunger," says Barbara. Perhaps this is the key to hiking that far. You just keep going and take it one day at a time. While there are lots of logistics and planning involved in a long trip, on a daily basis it comes down to walking, eating, and camping—just like you do on a two-day trip. I asked Mary what she liked best about backpacking, and she said, "There is no homework or school, and you meet a lot of really nice people. I love seeing all the woodland creatures like chipmunks and marmots, and the beautiful views from the trail."

As to advice for other children, Mary says that kids should backpack because "it is really fun and not that hard if you start out slow. It keeps your brain from turning to mush from watching TV and you meet a lot of new people. It is a great way to spend time with your friends. I love it, I will absolutely keep backpacking." Couldn't have said it better myself.

Where to Go, and Why

The key to backpacking with your kids is to pick a destination that is right for their capabilities. It should be a beautiful place that even an oblivious seven-year-old will appreciate. The difficult part is that this beautiful spot needs to a) be within walking distance for your little tykester, and b) not look like Grand Central Station at rush hour (or say, Lake Tahoe's Emerald Bay on a busy weekend). These conflicting goals are not always easy to rectify. If you have hiked and backpacked a lot yourself, it may be a challenge to get used to going to a place that might not be as exciting as you would like. It is worth making the compromise, however, to turn your children into backpackers. Just think, if they get excited about backpacking, in a few years, perhaps they will go with you to that awesome location you have always wanted to see. Try to put yourself in your kids' shoes, and figure out what they would find interesting on a hiking trip. Sure, the huge granite peaks and dramatic views are great and should be included if possible, but a child will be equally mesmerized by a frog squirting through the mud.

I have found that most seven- to nine-year-olds can handle a 3- to 5-mile hike in to the camping site, as long as it is not too steep. As they get older and more experienced, you can add a mile or two a year. I strongly recommend against setting out on a weeklong, 70-mile jaunt the first time you go backpacking with your child. Ease into it, make it fun, and they hopefully will want to do it again. Once you have made it to your extraordinary destination, schedule a layover day. This is the part of the trip that the kids

We made it!
Photo by
Denese Pillsbury

really enjoy, hanging out next to some lovely lake and spending a day doing as little as possible. You might get them to go for a short walk to a great viewpoint on the layover day, as long as they don't have to pick up that heavy backpack again until they are on their way home.

I live in Northern California, and my focus for hiking has been on the Sierra Nevada and other locations in California and Nevada. Some of my favorite places to go in this region include:

- In the San Francisco Bay Area, try Henry W. Coe State Park near Morgan Hill. This large park has lovely oak-covered hillsides and springtime wildflowers and water-falls. Several trips are on offer, with names like the Flat Frog Trail and Jackass Peak. What boy could resist hiking on Flat Frog Trail or to the top of Jackass Peak?

■ Near Graeagle, California, you can access Jamison, Wades, and Rock lakes in the Lakes Basin Recreational Area. The trail begins in the historical Plumas–Eureka State Park, a land of thick forest and small lakes in granite basins. In just a few easy miles of trail, you pass rusted remnants of gold mining operations, and then begin to pass lake after beautiful lake, perfect spots for family camping. Some of the biggest gold mining operations in the country began in this area in 1851 and continued for decades. The nearby town of Johnsville and the park headquarters museum provide a wealth of information on Plumas–Eureka's fascinating gold mining history.

■ Further north in California is Lassen Volcanic National Park and the Caribou Wilderness. The park's center-piece, Mt. Lassen, had a massive eruption in 1915, and the signs of its impact are still in evidence throughout the park. The Lassen vicinity has a number of short, lightly used trails taking you by several tree-ringed lakes that make for good camping spots. If your children have recently studied volcanic activity, this might be a great opportunity to bring their studies to life.

■ While the coast and the forest make great hiking lo-cales, I prefer heading into the high mountains. For older children, the Desolation Wilderness and the Tahoe Rim Trail at Lake Tahoe make excellent choices for short backpacking trips. While the access trails to Desolation can be a bit challenging, there are numerous

Hanging out at "Tim's Knob," overlooking Fontanillis Lake. This wonderful rock outcropping, which also provides views of Dicks Lake and Dicks Pass, was very unofficially named "Tim's Knob" by a group of Sierra Club hikers who were led by the author. Perhaps they felt guilty about sneaking their empty lunch bags and a couple of rocks into my backpack when I wasn't looking.

spectacular lakes within 5 miles of the various trailheads, including Genevieve and Crag lakes via Meeks Bay, or the Velma Lakes, Dicks Lake, and Fontanillis Lake via the two Emerald Bay trailheads. Lake Aloha in Desolation Wilderness is one of my favorite backpacking destinations. The huge lake sits right at the base of the Crystal Range and is surrounded by expansive flat granite slabs, a perfect place for kids to play. Read about my family's Lake Aloha adventures in chapter 6.

■ On the Tahoe Rim Trail, Star Lake (via the Armstrong Pass Trail) can be reached with a fairly strenuous 5-mile hike. Star Lake is a cool oasis along the drier eastern shore of Lake Tahoe. It sits just below Freel Peak, Jobs Sister, and Jobs Peak, the three highest mountains in the Lake Tahoe basin. From the Big Meadow trailhead of the Tahoe Rim Trail, close to South Lake Tahoe, you can reach Dardanelles and Round lakes within about 3 miles, and Showers Lake in 5 miles. All of these lakes are surrounded by granite or volcanic outcroppings and are loaded with fields of lupine and paintbrush in midsummer. If you are looking for more information on the Tahoe Rim Trail, pick up a copy of my book, *The Tahoe Rim Trail: A Complete Guide for Hikers, Mountain Bikers, and Equestrians,* published by Wilderness Press.

■ About 25 miles south of Lake Tahoe, at 8,592 feet in elevation, lies Carson Pass. Just a few miles south of the pass on a gentle trail, you reach Winnemucca Lake and Round Top Lake at the base of 10,364-foot Round Top mountain. The midsummer flower display on this trail is one of the best I have seen in the Sierra. It may even put a smile on a teenager. If you want a little more, you can go a few more miles past Round Top Lake to Fourth of July Lake, or trudge up to the top of Round Top for a stunning view all the way to Lake Tahoe.

■ The southern and central Sierra Nevada ranges, while higher and more dramatic than the more northerly peaks, also provide a few short, child-accessible hikes into prime terrain. The Virginia Lakes and Saddlebag Lake areas near Yosemite are two spots on the eastern side of the range that could be good choices for your family. From Saddlebag Lake you can hike an 8.5-mile loop that will take you past more than a dozen lakes. Even though you will be hiking at over 10,000 feet in elevation, the walking is easy, without a lot of ascent or descent. In the Mammoth Lakes area, you can hike out of Agnew Meadows to Ediza Lake or Thousand Island Lake. These two spectacular hikes take you to the middle of the high peaks without requiring a ton of effort. Finally, some of the best of California backpacking is found in Yosemite itself. While the park's beauty is only surpassed by its crowds, you can find some peace and quiet by hiking midweek and somewhere other than Yosemite Valley. Every kid should get to see Yosemite. One suggestion is to take the 3.7-mile hike from Tuolumne Meadows to Cathedral Lake. For more information on great backpacking choices in California, pick up a copy of *Backpacking California* by Wilderness Press.

There are a number of great backpacking spots to take children throughout the country. The Catskill and Adirondack mountains in New York State, the White and Green mountains of New Hampshire and Vermont, the Appalachian Trail, the Rocky Mountains, and the Cascades of Oregon and Washington are just a few. Contact your local hiking organizations and outdoor bookstores for more information on the best trails for children in your area.

As your children get older and become more experienced backpackers, it may take a longer trip to find the location that will really knock their socks off. Or perhaps the case is that you really want to go to the more exotic locales, and they are finally big enough to go there with you. Make plans to someday embark on a journey to a world-class hiking destination. A few very special places to go are:

> **John Muir Trail**—This 220-mile-long trail walks you through the heart of the High Sierra between Yosemite and the highest peak in the lower 48, Mt. Whitney. Much of the trip is above 10,000 feet, and all of it is awe inspiring.

Tahoe Rim Trail—The TRT completely circles Lake Tahoe on a 165-mile journey through two states (California and Nevada) and two mountain ranges. The views of Lake Tahoe from miles and miles of trail are the highlight, but spectacular mountain lakes in Desolation Wilderness are a special treat as well.

Colorado Trail—Beginning in Denver, the Colorado Trail travels 470 miles to Durango, Colorado. This hiking-and-mountain-biking trail goes from 5,500 feet to over 13,000 feet and passes close-by peaks above 14,000 feet in elevation. While it may not be an easy trail, it certainly is a beautiful one.

Lone Star Hiking Trail—Interested in a place to hike in the fall, winter, or spring? This may be it. It's a 130-mile trail in the Sam Houston National Forest, an hour north of Houston, Texas. The walking is relatively easy, unless you brave the unbearable heat of summer.

Long Path—It begins just north of New York City, and heads 345 miles north through the Gunks and the Catskills to just south of the state capital in Albany, New York. Who said you can't hike close to the city? Try it in the fall for the reds, yellows, and oranges of a Northeastern autumn.

Long Trail—One of the oldest trails in the United States, it covers the entire north-south distance of Vermont, from Massachusetts to Canada. This 270-mile trail journeys through the difficult but beautiful terrain of the Green Mountains. It is also an awesome choice if you are looking to hike through a dramatic fall color display.

Ozark Highlands Trail—Hike in the spring or fall on this 165-mile trail from Mountainburg to Gilbert, Arkansas.

Loaded with wildflowers and waterfalls, it is a special place in the Ozark Mountains.

Superior Hiking Trail—If you wish to go north, check out the 235-mile Superior Hiking Trail from Duluth, Minnesota, to Grand Portage, Minnesota. The trail follows a ridgeline high above the shores of Lake Superior.

Wonderland Trail—Considered one of America's most beautiful trails, the Wonderland Trail is a 95-mile loop around Mt. Rainier in Washington. Although it is certainly beautiful, you should be prepared for a strenuous trail with lots of swiftly moving creeks to cross.

These are just a few of the trails waiting anxiously to entice you into the wilds of America. For more information on America's long-distance hikes, pick up a copy of *Thru Hiker's Guide to America,* by E. Schlimmer. Take your pick out of this book or find another trail that strikes your fancy. Either way, you may be in for a once-in-a-lifetime experience. And if you are looking for a truly exotic adventure, how about taking your children abroad? Europe especially is geared toward hiking trips complete with comfortable huts to sleep in and the relaxing sound of cowbells.

CHAPTER 2

What?

You feel free! The sun's on your face and you have no obligations to school or anything. It's really quiet. Everything is so simple.

—Maiya Greenwood, 12

What to Do to Prepare for the Trip

The most important thing to do to prepare for your backpacking trip is to get your child excited about the adventure. Focus on the fun things that you will be doing, the things you will see, and how it will be an enjoyable family time. Be aware that children don't necessarily act as excited about nature as adults do. I have a tendency when I am hiking with my kids to exclaim every 100 yards, "Wow, look at that, it's a watchamacallit!," and the response is an eye roll that will make you dizzy, and a monotone, "yeah, that's great Dad . . . when's lunch?" Once the eye rolling is completed, however, they do find some of the little things especially interesting, like a tadpole, or a bug, a fish scooting under a log, a multicolored rock, or a blade of grass.

In order to increase their interest in the trip, work with them to decide where you would like to hike. Log on to the Internet and go to local outdoor stores and the library for information and maps on backpacking destinations. Pick up copies of *Outside* magazine and *Backpacker* magazine and go on their websites for backpacking information. Talk to Forest Service, National Park Service, or state park personnel and find out more about your chosen location. If there is a guidebook for the area you will be visiting, read through it, then bring along copies of the most pertinent pages on the trip.

Know the rules and regulations for the area you are visiting. Are there any fire restrictions or rules regarding bear canisters and bears? Is there a maximum number of people allowed in a group? Some areas limit the number of people allowed to camp, so advance reservations may be required. Be sure to plan ahead and do not wait until the last minute to get your permit.

Choose a place that will be enjoyable for your child, and that you feel he or she is capable of hiking to. Be honest with yourself as well, and make sure that you will not be overwhelmed by the difficulty of the trip. As stated before, it is best to start slow and work your way up to a longer jaunt.

Help your children physically prepare for the trip by taking them on walks and then short hikes. Your kids may surprise you with how physically strong they are, but often it may be the mental aspect of the trip that is more important to prepare for. Try to accentuate the positive, and make sure your child understands that most of the burden will be on you, the adult.

Learn about the plants you will be seeing on your hike. Pick up a field guide and on a walk with your child review a few of the more common plants that you will see in the wilderness. Start off in the spring by teaching little Jane about wildflowers. As the season progresses, move on to trees. While children often don't seem interested in the names of plants and animals, they really do feel proud that they can tell a fir tree from a pine, or the difference between a paintbrush and a lily.

While on walks, point out birds and squirrels and the other

Camp chores at Lake Aloha.

common animals that you will run into on your trip. If you see tracks in the snow or mud, try to determine what animal may have created them. Raccoons and deer have very distinctive footprints and your child may be able to identify these with a little help. This is a good time to talk about bears and how we avoid confrontations with them by keeping a clean camp, using a bear canister, and never leaving any food anywhere except inside a canister (more on bears later).

If you are not already certified, it is a good idea to take a first aid and CPR class. While the American Red Cross certifications are excellent, another alternative is to take a wilderness first aid course. These courses are geared specifically toward the emergencies that commonly occur in the wilderness. Perhaps it is selfish to make sure that your traveling companions are also first aid/CPR certified, but it is also smart. If every adult in your party has taken a first aid class, then there will always be someone there trained to handle the situation, even if you are the victim.

Make one more call to the local park ranger or Forest Service official for the area you will be hiking before your trip. This will give you a chance to make sure no last-minute changes have occurred to the trail. A bridge out? Too much snow? You can also see if there are any newly imposed fire restrictions. Often during dry periods fire restrictions are instituted, including prohibitions on campfires or even total closure of some areas to camping.

Now that your children are prepared and excited about hiking and backpacking, you have chosen a good place to go, and you have introduced them to a few of the basics of nature, it's time to take the next step and figure out what you need to bring with you on your trip.

WHAT COMES ALONG? MORE IMPORTANT, WHAT STAYS AT HOME?

The biggest problem with backpacking with kids is that they have to carry stuff and then walk up hills with all that stuff on their backs. I know that sounds simplistic, but ask them, and they will tell you: "I like it once we get there, it is just the walking uphill with that really, really heavy pack on that I don't like. Can't you carry it for me!?" Of course you wish you could carry their "really, really heavy pack" that weighs about ¼ the weight of yours. While some children just grin and bear it, most have brought the subtle non-ending whine to an art form while trudging uphill to your destination. I remember my daughter on her first trip managed to coerce us into stopping about a hundred times so she could tie her shoelaces. Eventually, I did begin to understand that shoelaces, for some strange reason, only became untied on the uphill climbs. Given that this may be one of the biggest issues you have to deal with in taking your brood on a trip, it behooves you to figure out how to keep their load light. Or at least their shoelaces tied. The key is not to remove things from their packs, and then put them in yours, but to lower the weight of both of your packs. It is time to learn what you really need to bring and bring only that.

What Style of Backpacker Are You?

You have two primary (and conflicting) goals when filling up your backpack: 1) bring everything you need, and 2) keep it light. A better way of looking at it is: bring only what you will need and nothing more. We can come up with a million catchphrases, but it is still easier said than done. Experienced backpackers spend trip after trip zeroing in on the best way to lower weight without leaving out something they will really need.

There are basically three schools of backpacking. The old-school method was to bring everything you might possibly need and grunt and groan your way up the hill. You wanted to make sure that you were not left without any of the comforts of home, so you brought the entire home. If you survived the hike to your destination, you had a ton of great stuff at your camp, most of which you did not need, or you could certainly have done without. These were the days when people brought in cast iron pans and canned food, heavy, bulky clothing and way too much of it. I remember reading a book about the first guy to hike the Pacific Crest Trail. He hiked over 2,600 miles with a 70–80-pound pack, wearing blue jeans! These days many long-distance hikers carry packs that weigh 25 pounds or less.

Fortunately, the old school died and was buried about 20 years ago. It probably died of cardiac arrest at the top of a steep hill. Some people still are not aware that it is dead, but those of us in the backpacking business are doing our best to put the final nail in its coffin.

The second school of backpacking is lightweight backpacking. It is more of a balanced approach with all the basic necessities covered, but keeping it as light as possible. The key to this method is to carefully evaluate the trip and only bring what you really need, then go back and try to cut a few things out. Once you have the list of what you really need, start investigating how to do the job with the lightest gear possible. For clothing this means lightweight synthetic fabrics and fleece (which will also keep you warm and dry). For toiletries, it means bringing a small toothpaste tube, a small tube of sunscreen, half a roll of toilet paper and only the amount of medications and supplies you will need. The biggest category for weight and space is camping supplies. Tents and sleeping bags need to be as lightweight as possible. You should only have to bring one bowl and cup each (some only bring a cup), and one heavy-duty plastic spoon.

Food can really add a lot of weight unless it is closely evaluated and planned. At home, remove as much packaging as possible and then repack your food in lightweight Ziploc bags. Bring only the food that you will eat. This means sitting down and planning out a menu for the entire trip, and then throwing in just a little extra. While cooked food is great, for safety's sake be sure to take enough food that doesn't require cooking as well, in case your stove doesn't work (yes, that does happen, especially if you are traveling with me).

The third school of backpacking is called ultralight. Originally developed for fast-moving, long-distance backpacking trips, ultralight hiking's goal is to eliminate as much weight as possible and get down to the very bare minimum. There seems to be some sort of competition out there as to who can hike with the least amount of weight. On web hiking forums or along the trail the tit for tat has gotten to the point where I expect to soon hear, "Oh, yeah! Well I carry a fanny pack with a space blanket, a water bottle, a headlamp, and a pound of dried oatmeal. My pack weighs two pounds. I drink out of streams, eat wild berries, and sleep under

One happy camper, and one not-so-happy camper.

my space blanket. The only problem is that since I have no sleeping bag, I can't stop hiking. I did the John Muir Trail in five days. If I could just get out of this hospital bed I'd do it again!" The difference between ultralight and light backpacking, in my opinion, comes down to comfort level. Ultralight hikers are more comfortable while hiking along the trail, light hikers are more comfortable once they stop hiking and get to camp.

While sometimes it gets carried to an extreme, most of what ultralight hikers are pushing for is a very good thing. Trying to hike truly ultralight with children, however, is difficult and may be unsafe. It is my understanding that what makes ultralight hiking lighter comes down to a few pieces of gear:

> Tent—Many ultralight hikers carry small, super-light tents that can be put up with hiking poles, while others just use a lightweight bivy sack or tarp. While this tech-

nique can work great for adults, in my experience most children appreciate the feeling of security that they get from a tent. Tents also keep out the rain and mosquitoes, either of which can ruin a trip for a child.

Stoves—Ultralight hikers often use a small alcohol-burning stove, sometimes inside an old tuna can, instead of a regular backpacking stove.

Water Purification—To reduce weight they replace a water filter with chemical treatment (iodine or other water purifier). Again, for an individual this may be a great weight saver, but for a family it is very nice to be able to filter lots of good-tasting water, instead of waiting for iodine to work.

Food Storage—Instead of a bear canister, ultralight hikers use rope to hang food from trees. While this may work well in areas with few bears or other critters, I have found a bear canister to be well worth the extra weight in areas where bears are common. They are also effective at keeping out marmots and squirrels.

Lightweight Everything—Ultralight aficionados sit down and go over every item, counting ounces carefully. When it comes to sleeping bags, clothing, and whatever else they put into a backpack, the primary goal is to reduce ounces. While this makes sense, it can also be more expensive.

Packs—Finally, some ultralight hikers have discovered that if you can reduce the total volume of all the things you need to put in your backpack, you can also reduce the size and thus the weight of the backpack itself.

Using as many of the ultralight backpacking ideas that you feel comfortable with is a good idea. When you purchase new gear, try to make it as light as possible. Carry only what you need, and always focus on lowering weight. Try to incorporate gear in your pack that serves more than one purpose. If you are an accomplished ultralight backpacker, however, you may want to take a few steps toward the heavier side to increase comfort and safety for your children. I believe your kids are well served by being able to sleep in a tent, drink filtered water, and eat hot, comforting food prepared with a lightweight backpacking stove. While lowering weight is a worthwhile goal, you also want to make sure that the child's backpacking experience is a positive one, so he or she will want to do it again.

What to Bring

CAMPING SUPPLIES

Don't be a gearhead, but head for the right gear. Spend the time to learn all you need to know about gear, plan carefully, and purchase the best that you can afford. Never forget, however, that hiking and backpacking is about enjoying nature, not about what fancy doohickies you can use while you are in the mountains. While there are certainly some items that are worth springing the extra cash for, it is not necessary to spend an extra hundred dollars to save two ounces in your pack. Escape from materialism, focus on the journey. There are whole books that focus on backpacking gear. While they are great books with a ton of research behind them, they are outdated about 15 minutes after they are published (actually even before they are published). While I am attempting to give you a general idea on the basics of camping gear, I have tried to steer away from a discussion of the best brands or types in each category (with a few exceptions, like when I get really excited about a product). For the latest and greatest in technology, fabrics, or techniques, your favorite outdoor stores and magazines, as well as the Internet, are the best places to go.

Backpack—The world of gear begins with a backpack. Make sure it fits. Try on several different models and load them up with the volume and weight that you would carry on a trip. This will help you to understand what it will feel like on the trail, which is more important than what it feels like in the store. Don't scrimp on a cheap, department store backpack; your shoulders, hips, and back will pay the price on the trail. If you are not sure whether you want to do a lot of backpacking, rent or borrow a good pack first before making an investment. What about the pack for Junior? If it is his first trip, a large day pack may work, or even a school pack if it is fairly good sized. Once the kids get bigger, and it looks like backpacking is in their future, they will need to be fitted for their own packs. My children borrow my old Dana Bomb Pack, which is a large day pack/small overnight pack, and it now fits them well as a full backpack. Of course the first time my younger daughter wore it, the question was, "Which is bigger, Hannah or the backpack?"

Once you have the right pack, figure out how it works. Most packs have all kinds of straps and clips that are adjusted to fit the individual hiker. Have your retailer adjust them to fit you, but plan on making frequent adjustments as you hike to tighten and loosen the straps to provide the most comfort. You want to start out with your hip belt nice and snug, and then tighten up the shoulder straps. Often on longer hikes I will start out with a tighter hip belt and a looser shoulder strap and then partway through the hike I will tighten the shoulder straps to give my hips a bit of a break. Also make sure that the hip belt is on correctly. Once I complained to the expert at my favorite outdoor store

All it needs is a human to carry it.

that my hips were hurting after a recent five-day trip. I thought for sure something must have been wrong with the pack. She looked at the pack and softly said, "Perhaps it would be more comfortable if you had the belt on right side up." Apparently the upside-down hiker on the face of the buckle was not enough to give me a clue.

Sleeping bag—Sleeping bags are divided into two types, synthetic and down. I prefer the soft, warm feel of down, although if it gets wet, it is a bad, bad thing (because it takes forever to dry). While most hikers are dedicated to down, others find that synthetics have improved to the point that they are a good alternative. The next three factors to consider when purchasing a bag are: How much do you want to spend? How heavy will the bag be? How cold will it be where you are hiking? Bags are rated based on temperature. A 20-degree bag is designed to be comfortable down to 20 degrees. The manufacturers are quick to point out that these ratings are for comparison purposes only. They cannot guarantee that every person will be comfortable at 20 degrees, but it is a system that for most people works well.

I would suggest purchasing the lightest bag that meets your temperature range and budget. Most parents cannot afford to provide their children with top-of-the-line products to go backpacking. For younger children, a synthetic bag may be the way to go as they are cheaper and washable; on the other hand, they are often heavier. If you are going to splurge for one high-quality backpacking item for a Christmas or birthday present for your children, however, a sleeping bag may be the one. Get a quality built, lightweight bag. It will last them a long time, and they can use it not only for backpacking, but when they get to college it will be available to crash at some friend's pad after that wild party. Red is probably a good color as it will hide the wine stains. Oh, sorry, this is probably more information than any parent wants to think about.

Sleeping pads—There are two basic styles, foam pads, which are light and cheap, but not very comfy, and inflating pads (Thermarest is the best known) that inflate up to about 1 inch thick and provide for a more comfortable sleep than foam. Inflating pads are heavier and more expensive than foam pads, but I have found my Thermarest pad is essential to get a good, or at least better, night of sleep out on the cold, hard ground. Inflating pads insulate you better from the cold and are softer than a regular foam pad. A patch kit is a necessity for inflating pads, as I can say from experience that they sometimes spring holes and leak.

Stove—Recently, I acquired a Jetboil backpacking stove, and I think it is the best thing for backpacking since synthetic fabrics. The pot/burner/canister are all attached so you don't have to bring extra pots or fuel. You don't even need a match as it lights with a little clicker like a gas BBQ. It boils water so fast that once you start it you better hurry up and get that oatmeal in the bowl, because it is going to be boiling soon. There are a number of other options for types of stove, each with its advantages and disadvantages. Some hikers prefer lightweight, white gas stoves. The gas is cheaper and lighter than canisters, especially for longer trips, and if you are cooking or simmering food, as opposed to boiling water, the stoves have their advantages. Be sure to find a stove that is light, easy to operate, and does not take up a lot of space. As with everything else on this list, go to a good outdoor/hiking store for the latest and greatest.

Tent—A lightweight backpacking tent is best. I would not recommend the $25 A-frame special at Wal-Mart that looks like leftover army camouflage. Like the backpack, if you are not sure your kid will be a hiker, borrow a good tent from someone first, rather than buying the wrong one. If you are hiking with a partner you need at least a two-person tent, and many so-called two-person tents can be snug for one, let alone two, so make sure you see the tent all set up (it's even better to get inside it) before you buy it. There are a ton of different brands and styles; choose the one that works best for you (and of course that you think looks the coolest.

Tent beside the lake.

Mine looks like a mosquito, which the kids love). *If* the
weather is really nice and the forecast does not show a
chance of rain, *and* you are past mosquito season, you
might be able to get away without a tent—unless you
are hiking with me. If it only rains three times in a summer, I assure you that those will be the days I'm on a
backpacking trip. Ask my kids. In fact, if you would like
to determine whether it will rain when you are going
backpacking, just give me a call and find out whether
I am out hiking. If I am hiking, and you are going to
the same place, bring the tent and rain fly. While lots
of experienced adult backpackers can get away without a tent, most children like the privacy that a tent
provides. And besides, if all else fails you can use the
tent for "time-out." Whatever you do, set up the tent
at your house before your trip. If you arrive in the dark

Girls always enjoy filtering water.

and can't figure out how to set it up, it will put a bit of a damper on your spirits.

Water filter—The water in the woods may not be safe to drink. Although some hikers drink water from mountain streams without getting sick, they are playing a game of water roulette. I assure you, kids with *Giardia* (an intestinal parasite waiting peacefully for you in untreated water) are not fun, so treat all your water before consuming it. Water should be filtered, treated chemically with iodine or a similar product, or boiled. For more information, see the "Water" section in chapter 4. The easiest method is to purchase a lightweight water filter designed for backpacking. Your outdoor retailer can give you a rundown on the different models. They are reasonably priced and, if treated gently, last a long time.

First aid kit—You can make your own or purchase one through an outdoor retailer. A number of different types and sizes of first aid kits have been developed for backpacking use. The trick is to get the smallest and lightest kit that contains what you are likely to need. While there is the remote possibility that you may need something from one of those humongous first aid kits that weighs 10 pounds, it is best to leave those behemoths in the hospital emergency room where they belong. Based on my experience, and the recommendations of first aid instructors, I suggest you include the following in your first aid kit: Hand sanitizer, antibacterial wipes, several pieces of gauze and tape, several Band-Aids of different sizes, an Ace bandage, superglue (can be used to hold a cut together), iodine or other solution for irrigation of a wound, safety pins, antibiotic cream (Neosporin), antacid (Tums or Pepto-Bismol—which also can serve as an antidiarrheal), temporary dental filling material or kit if you have dental fillings, knife, scissors, tweezers (if they have a magnifying glass, all the better), credit card or driver's license (for removing bee stingers), Benadryl (diphenhydramine) for allergies and itching. If you are highly allergic to bee stings or anything else, also bring an EpiPen, space blanket, electrolyte solution (a small container of powder, something that an exhausted or dehydrated person can use to quickly replenish fuels; one highly effective brand is Emergen-C), ibuprofen or Tylenol, plastic bags, safety mask or shield (for CPR), plastic gloves, and of course—duct tape! Obviously, if you are already packing such items as iodine, a knife, and duct tape, you do not need duplicates in the first aid kit. While having a kit is important, equally important is to take a first aid/ CPR course to learn how to use it.

Camping Supplies List

Make a copy of this list and refer to it often when getting ready for a trip. See also the "Clothing and Toiletries List" and the "Food List," later in this chapter.

Backpack

Backpacking tent and rain fly

Sleeping pad and repair kit

Sleeping bag

First aid kit/supplies

Backpacking pillow (or pillowcase to use your clothes as a pillow)

Stove, fuel, pot (separate or all-in-one unit)

Water filter and chemical tablets as a backup

Water bottles and/or hydration pack (Camelback)

Trowel (pooper-scooper)

Bowl

Cup

Utensils (spork or spoon)

Sharp knife or Swiss Army knife

Compass

Headlamp or flashlight (extra batteries and bulbs; kids love headlamps)

Map (and/or guidebook pages)

Field guides (luxury item, but nice for teaching children about plants)

Deck of cards (also luxury, but if it rains, a sanity saver)

Lightweight book (see suggestions in the appendix)

Camera and extra battery if it is a long trip

Lightweight rope

Lighter and/or waterproof matches

Duct tape (see "Ten Things to Do with Duct Tape" later in this chapter)

Bear canister

Space blanket (emergency)

Water scoop (if you don't have a water filter, to scoop water into your container; not needed if you bring a water filter)

Whistle

Writing journal, pen(s)

Ziploc bags (for journal, camera, maps, toiletries, etc.)

Glasses and sunglasses (if you use both, don't forget the pair you are not wearing!)

Several large heavy-duty plastic garbage bags (to keep things dry if it rains)

In a small plastic bag, driver's license, credit card, $40 cash, car key, health insurance card

Bandanna

Food for the amount of time you will be gone

Clothing (see the "Clothing and Toiletries List" later in this chapter)

Eleven Things to Do with the Bandanna

Ah, the bandanna. It's a wonderful thing. The only thing more versatile than a bandanna is duct tape.

1. Wear it as a scarf on your head to keep the sun and bugs off your neck. Wet it and you will not only feel cool, but look cool as well. In a nerdy, ex-hippie kind of way.

2. Small towel

3. Pot holder

4. Dish towel

5. Loincloth/emergency bathing suit

6. Bandage

7. Something to sit on to keep your butt dry

8. Emergency flag

9. Handkerchief

10. Camping partner swatter

11. Protects the allergy-sufferer from pollen, mold, etc. . . . (worn over your mouth, à la cowboy bandito)

LUXURIES YOU CAN BRING FOR A SHORT TRIP WITH THE KIDS

Thermarest chair kit—You fold in your Thermarest pad, and it makes a comfy chair

Binoculars

Fanny or day pack for layover days

Small, lightweight game or toy of some sort

CLOTHES

The mantra is to bring everything you need, and absolutely nothing more. If you don't have backpacking clothes already, then you need to know what to buy. The primary principle to remember when putting together a backpacking (or hiking, or any other outdoor sport for that matter) wardrobe is layering. Instead of one large fleece jacket, take several lightweight layers, and make sure to bring only synthetic fabrics. If you are a regular cross-country skier, biker, or hiker, you may already have many of the pieces of clothing you will need in your closet. For spring, summer, and fall hiking you (and Junior) need:

> **A pair of hiking shorts**—Steer clear of cotton. There are some really cool synthetic shorts with chamois sewn into the waistband for added comfort and to prevent chafing. I like a pair of convertible pants that I can wear as short or long pants depending upon the time of day, temperature, number of mosquitoes, and whether the trail is overgrown. Some shorts can double for bathing suits if you feel so inclined to wear one.

> **Lightweight synthetic shirt**—Bring this instead of a cotton T-shirt. It wicks away moisture, while keeping you warm and dry. Its one downfall is that it does tend to stink after you sweat in it, but it washes and dries quickly on a granite rock. When cotton gets wet, which it will when you are grunting along with 40 pounds on your back, it (and therefore you) can become cold and clammy. Or if the temperature is high, you will be a soaking-wet sponge. Stay away from cotton. This is your first layer of three.

> **Warm fleece shirt**—A medium-weight shirt will keep you warm in the early morning and evening, but not so warm that it will be heavy and bulky. This is your second or middle layer.

> **Waterproof shell**—Popular for biking, these lightweight shells should keep the rain out, while letting the sweat escape. This is your third or outer layer that will also

help you to stay warm on a cold evening or early morning.

Waterproof pants—Talk to your retailer about pants that keep the water out without trapping the sweat in. See waterproof shell above. If you are concerned about weight, and rain doesn't appear to be an issue, this is one item of clothing you might leave at home. Especially if you have a pair of convertible short/pants to keep you warm at night.

Underwear—While cotton will work, you will be more comfortable on a long hike with underwear made from synthetic fabric. Many hikers prefer going commando (which means bringing no underwear at all, a nice weight savings).

Two pairs of synthetic or wool socks—Be sure these are not cotton. Nothing causes blisters as quickly as cotton socks. Some people prefer one layer of medium-weight hiking socks made of a comfortable fiber such as Smart-Wool, while others like to hike with a thin inner liner and an outer pair of wool or synthetic fabric. Take some hikes ahead of time and see what is most comfortable for you.

Sun-shielding hat—Some prefer baseball type hats, but more coverage for your neck is provided by a sun hat with a brim that goes all the way around your head.

Hiking boots—While many hikers are comfortable in sneakers, others prefer high-backed, heavyweight hiking boots. Most will find the best satisfaction somewhere in between. Be sure and take a few hikes with your chosen footwear, and make sure they are comfortable before hitting the trail for a several-day trip. It is also important that you test your boots with a heavy pack on. Shoes

Make a copy of this list, and refer to it often when getting ready for a trip. Items are grouped into three sections.

What to Wear at the Start

Hiking shorts/ convertible pants

Synthetic underwear

Shirt

SmartWool or synthetic socks

Sun hat

Sunscreen

Midweight hiking boots

What to Bring in the Pack

Warm fleece shirt

Lightweight rain shell

Extra pair of socks

Rain pants

Sport sandals

Depending upon the trip you *may* want to bring an extra pair

of shorts that can double as a swim suit and a cotton T-shirt just to wear around camp at the end of the day.

If you are sensitive to cold, are hiking between October and

May, or hiking in a very cold place you may want to add the following:

Fleece or wool hat

Gloves

Warm jacket

Long johns

Toiletries

Toothbrush

Toothpaste (small tube)

Vitamins and medications (Tylenol, anti-diarrhea medicine, vitamin C, multivitamins)

Sunscreen (small tube)

Biodegradable all-purpose soap (washing dishes, doing laundry) and scrubby sponge

For women: sanitary napkins (can also be used as bandages) or tampons

Toilet paper (small roll or half roll)

Mosquito repellent

Baby wipes (to clean up and sanitize)

Lip balm and vaseline product for chafing prevention or an alternative lip balm

that work just fine on a short trip with a light pack can cause problems with a heavy pack over rough terrain. Today's boots should not take as long to "work in" as the big clunkier boots often used by old-school hikers.

The longer the trip, the more important it is to have the right shoes. Almost nothing can make a trip more miserable than blistered feet.

Around camp shoes—I recommend sport sandals like Tevas. They are lightweight, good for walking through creek crossings, and comfy to hang around camp in. I do not recommend flip-flops, because they are dangerous for your feet amongst all the boulders and bushes, or sneakers, because they are heavy and if you use them to walk over wet boulders or along the shoreline, they will get wet, and stay wet.

Remember, when it comes to putting together your clothing for a trip: It is better not to smell like a rose than to carry too much of a load. If absolutely necessary you can wash some clothes at your camp, but don't bring too many clothes! Repeat after me: DO NOT BRING TOO MANY CLOTHES!

FOOD—AN OVERVIEW

Everybody has his or her own ideas when it comes to developing a list of food to bring. Your food supply must do the following:

1. Be lightweight.

2. Not take up too much room in your pack or bear canister.

3. Taste good.

4. Fill you up and provide the nutrients and energy you will need on a backpacking trip.

5. Stay fresh for the period of your trip without being refrigerated.

6. Be easy to prepare. To me, easy to prepare means either you eat it as it is, or you boil water. The only dishes

I want to be cleaning are bowls, spoons, and mugs. Many backpackers enjoy more elaborate backcountry cooking. There are several books available that provide details on how to prepare gourmet meals over a backpacking stove. Personally, I would rather spend more time staring at the clouds, but many people really enjoy cooking in the backcountry. The good news is that if you hike far enough and you are in a beautiful place, all food tastes great!

Some items that will work fine on a one- or two-night trip will take up too much space, will spoil, or will weigh too much on a longer trip. In the list below, you will find an "s" (short) next to food that is probably best suited to a short trip or the first day of a longer trip.

Looking for new ideas for food? Take a slow stroll through Trader Joe's. If you have backpacking on your mind, it is amazing what you will find. They not only have the widest selection of gorp you can imagine, but a lot of other healthy foods that will stay in good condition on the trail. What is gorp? It comes in different varieties, but usually contains dried fruit and nuts, and sometimes crackers and chocolate. Try a few different types before your trip to find your favorite.

For a wide selection of dehydrated backpacking food, go to your favorite outdoor retailer. Where do you find the best new ideas? Try hiking with friends and see what they pull out of their backpacks. Avocado? It never entered my mind until I tasted that bit of lush greenness on a sunny afternoon next to a mountain lake. Experiment and try new things before you go on the trip so you know what works. You will be amazed that foods you never considered as backpack food make perfect meals in the backcountry.

If you are planning on backpacking on a regular basis, you

Food List

Pick and choose from this list, and add your own ideas. It is OK to eat "lunch" food for dinner or breakfast, and vice versa. In fact, when camping, kids should eat candy for breakfast and eggs for dinner. They should dine on dandelions and fish. Cereal with Tang. Chocolate, lots of chocolate. Whatever strikes their fancy and keeps them laughing.

Breakfast:

Instant Oatmeal	Cold cereal	Tang
Dried Fruit	Breakfast bars or Pop-Tarts	Hot chocolate, tea, coffee
Peaches or other fruit in plastic containers (S)	Powdered milk	

Lunch:

Salami	Jelly (borrow some from a restaurant the morning of your trip)	Ramen
Hard cheese (Parmesan, Gruyère, Romano)		Dry soup in a package or plastic bag
Cheddar cheese (S)	Tuna (in foil pouches)	Macaroni and cheese
Tortillas (white or whole wheat flour only)	Avocado (S)	Beef jerky
Bagels (S)	Crackers (in hard container to protect from smashing)	Gorp
Peanut butter (it comes in a tube)	Sandwich (S, first lunch)	

may want to consider purchasing a dehydrator. These inexpensive machines will dry vegetables, fruits, and even meat for taking with you on a trip. It is often difficult to get your vegetables on a backpacking trip (sorry, Mom), and dehydrators are an easy way to make that happen. Of course, this may not make your kids happy, as there are many children who love backpacking expressly because they don't have to eat their vegetables (sorry, Mom).

Dinner:

Dehydrated gourmet backpack meals—These come in a huge variety to fit just about every taste. Most are pasta- or rice-based, with dried meat and vegetables. There are even breakfast and dessert dishes. Be sure to try them out before the trip, especially if you are sensitive to spices. It is disconcerting to realize after the first bite that the stuff in your mouth that is your only dinner feels like it is on fire and brings tears to your eyes.

Dehydrated products: vegetables, fruit, jerky.

Couscous

Ramen

Pasta dishes

Gorp

Snacks:

Gorp

Candy—Hard candy will hit the spot. Chocolate tastes good, but in warm temperatures it will melt and make a mess. Try M&Ms, because as you know from watching too much TV, they melt in your mouth, not in your backpack.

Energy and granola bars

Fruit roll-ups

Cookies

I have experienced a few dietary horror stories such as corn tortillas, which quickly turn to chips when smashed into a pack, or rice cakes, which turn into little kernels of rice when smashed into a pack, but in general from experimentation come great ideas. Perhaps my trips would be more enjoyable if I did some of the experimentation at home before I stuffed what was soon to become useless food in my backpack.

Hungry babies like to hang out near the bear canister. Photo by Paul Honeywell.

Remember, you are camping with kids. You're better off feeding them something they like and having them eat it than attempting to give them healthy stuff that they don't like and risk their not eating it, or not eating enough of it. If you want to work on improving their diet, home is the place to do it. In the woods, they just need to eat basically good stuff and enough of it.

What to Put in Your Child's Pack

How much of that big pile of stuff sitting in your living room can you foist off on your child? Somewhere in between making her your Sherpa and letting her skip along without carrying anything. What they can bring depends upon their age, strength, and physical conditioning. I have given a few rough estimates below, but of course it varies with each child and the length of the trip.

6–8 YEARS OLD: FIRST TRIP

Try to keep it under 10 pounds:

Wear: Shorts, T-shirt, socks

Carry: Small backpack

Long pants

Long-sleeved shirt, preferably fleece

Rain shell

Water bottle or hydration system

Sleeping bag or pad (you carry the other)

Extra pair of socks

Snack or candy

Bandanna (for dipping in creeks to cool off)

8–10 YEARS OLD: SECOND OR LATER TRIP

All of the above plus:

Small first aid kit

Both sleeping bag and pad

Today's lunch

Bowl and cup, spoon

Toothbrush, toothpaste, medicines

Camp shoes

11–15 YEARS OLD

All of the above plus:

Stove or the water filter (you carry the other)

There are websites galore detailing thousands of different things you can do with duct tape. (I know, I know there are thousands of websites on everything. What did all these people do with themselves before the Internet?) Duct tape, the silver miracle product. And now it even comes in a variety of colors. If you asked 100 long-distance backpackers what the most important thing they brought on their trip was, many would extol the virtues of the lowly duct tape. Which of course may be more of a comment on long-distance backpackers than duct tape, but I digress. Take it along and you may come up with a plethora of uses. Here are a few of my suggestions:

1. Repair a broken hiking or tent pole. By the way, wrapping it around your hiking pole is a good way to carry duct tape.

2. Use as a bandage (to hold down a bandanna of course) or blister preventer. It works pretty well on removing warts as well, or to use as a finger splint.

3. Repair a hole in a backpack or tent, or replace a broken zipper.

4. To shut the little bugger up. Just kidding, one should never hurt the little brat's self-esteem. Just consider it a "time out" opportunity for him to reconsider his actions while the duct tape is gently placed over his mouth. It can also be used to tie him to a tree, but again, I am just kidding, just kidding. Just because someone did it to me when I was a child doesn't mean the pattern has to continue. Besides, it is a sibling's job to tie you to the tree, not your parents'.

5. Seal plastic bags, say, the one containing used toilet paper, for example.

6. Cover up that hole in your pants, shirt, hat, or brain.

7. Reattach a detached sole to your shoe (I am not sure if it does anything about your spiritual soul; for that one, you're on your own), or keep the shoe together if your shoelace died.

8. Repair a broken stove, cooking pot, or plastic spoon—in other words, allow you to eat. If all else fails you can even use it to construct a bowl.

9. Construct a rope to use whatever you need a rope for while backpacking (tying stuff or removing dead bodies).

10. And when you return to the trailhead, repairing the hose on your car that the marmot has eaten through (might be a good reason to return to your car before dark).

16 AND OVER

Divide up the food and other items so that your child is taking about 60 percent of what you are taking, depending upon their size. You could still carry the bear canister, but have them carry a good portion of the food, perhaps the tarp for the tent. You should be hiking longer distances as well, so it is important that your bag not be too heavy and that you are sharing the load. Hopefully, by this time your child is a strapping teenager with several trips under his or her belt, and he or she is ready and willing (well, that might be a stretch) to carry his share of the load. The key to making this work is to evaluate the overall weight very carefully and work on reducing it. The good news is that if you are splitting up the weight equally you should both have fairly lightweight loads.

What You Don't Need in Your Backpack (and the Alternative)

Or at least you don't need it bad enough to carry it on your back for miles.

Body soap (smell or swim)

Washcloth (bandanna)

Big towel (bandanna)

Deodorant and cosmetics (smell)

Radio (oh, pleeasse!)

Wallet (put the essentials in a Ziploc bag)

A whole set of keys (car key)

Hairdryer (no electricity)

Hairbrush (bring a comb or nothing if your hair is short)

GPS (map)

Iron skillet (lightweight pot)

Canned food (freeze-dried or dehydrated)

Sierra cup (plastic mug)

Big honking knife with twenty gadgets on it (small lightweight knife with a pair of scissors)

Down parka (layers)

Cardboard box meals (remove the boxes and put in plastic Ziploc)

Little Janey's favorite stuffed bear (try to sneak it out when she is not looking)

Ten pounds of gorp (the amount you will actually eat)

Whole magazine (you can bring in the remains of one lightweight magazine with all the ads ripped out)

Hardcover book (soft cover)

Bra (sports bra)

Woman's bathing suit top (sports bra or nothing depending upon location and your comfort factor)

Tape recorder (small notebook)

CHAPTER 3

Backpacking with Infants and Toddlers

Roasting marshmallows, sleeping in tents, making mud pies,
finding a river to swim in, hiding behind bushes to scare
people, and finding flowers to give to my mom.
—Aubrey Clement, 6

I like jumping off cliffs and climbing volcanoes.
—Colby Clement, 3

So, you and your partner have been enjoying backpacking together for years. A two-week trip into the wilderness has always been a wonderful experience that you look forward to every year. It's all fun, you love it out there and want to backpack forever. Now, you went and had a kid. What were you thinking? Oh, yeah, you were thinking how special it would be to have another person in your life and you now have the opportunity to teach him or her all about the mountains and the joys of backpacking. It's ok, babies can backpack. In fact, they have been hauled around on their parents' backs or chests for millions of years. If you are ready to take the plunge and bring your baby or toddler on an overnight trip, however, you need to be aware of a few issues that older children don't bring with them.

Bring your infant to the High Sierra, the whole family will love it. Photo by Paul Honeywell

First, parent #1 is going to carry the baby, and parent #2 is going to carry their gear plus most of the stuff that parent #1 usually carries. Sure, the parent who is carrying the child can take a few things in the baby backpack, but the bulk of the weight needs to go on the back of the mule, I mean the parent who isn't carrying the little one. In case you haven't figured it out yet, this means you may want to keep the distance traveled down to a few miles, and long steep climbs over passes are probably not recommended. Also, it is extremely difficult to take an infant or toddler on a trip with just one parent. I haven't figured out how to do it, which might explain why I didn't take my kids out until they were about seven years old.

One possibility if you have only one parent willing or able to take the trip is to bring along another adult who is agreeable to taking a portion of the burden. This saintly individual (or insane individual?) could be a friend or relative who likes hanging out with you and your child. Even if you have two parents ready to take the trip, another adult along can be helpful. For such largesse the parents will owe dinner, a six-pack of beer, and eternal gratitude.

The mule parent needs a large pack capable of carrying all of the stuff required by both parents. The parent carrying the child needs a good-quality child carrier that is designed to carry children, with padded waist belts and shoulder straps. Your flimsy little kid pack that was $5 at the garage sale is probably not the one to use.

Second, what are the special things to think about when traveling in the woods with a baby? Let's start with the food. Breast-feeding can be a very good thing. It is much easier to carry your weight on your, eh, front, than on your back. For the rest of the food, or if your breast-feeding days are over, try to repackage food so it is as light as possible. Get rid of the glass containers and other heavy packaging. While keeping a well-balanced diet that he or she will eat, spend some time planning out the meals for several days. Remember to work at reducing not only the weight of the food, but its volume as well. All of the food for all three of you needs to fit in the bear canister.

Third, diapers are the only thing I can think of that weigh more at the end of a backpacking trip than at the beginning. Gauge how many you will need for the trip and develop a method to keep the dirty ones away from the rest of your stuff. To dispose of a dirty diaper, the first step is to take the poop and put it in a cathole, and then store the used diaper in a large Ziploc bag (for more information on catholes, go to Top Ten Ways to Be Good in the Woods, in chapter 4). Fold the accumulated Ziplocs into a bigger bag with some sort of odor reducer like baking soda and then duct tape it all together tightly. You don't want the scent attracting animals. You can also put the used diapers inside of a Ursack, which is a tough, flexible sack designed to keep bears and other animals out. Or you should put it in your bear canister. It is probably a good idea to

Happy babies make happy mommies! Photo by Paul Honeywell

make sure it doesn't leak all over your food. Nothing like having used diapers in your bear canister to make you forget about fixing lunch. If you bring a dog along, have it carry out the used diapers. Now that is a dog that is earning its keep.

Studies have shown that more hikers get sick from poor hygiene than from contaminated water. Usually this poor hygiene is just a failure to wash your hands after going to the bathroom, so with a baby especially, practice good sanitation by washing your hands frequently and using antibacterial lotion.

Next, the good news is that baby clothes are small and light. While you certainly need enough clothes to get through the trip, the emphasis does not need to be on keeping him or her clean the whole time. Infants will get really, really dirty, so you might as well carry fewer clothes and live with it. As they get older, you will realize that kids think one of the best things about backpacking is that you get really, really dirty. That said, when choosing a site to camp

Peekaboo! Photo by Karen Honeywell

it is a good idea to find a place that isn't dusty. The one piece of clothing not to forget is a sun hat. Most likely you will be exposed to the sun for most of the day so be extra careful to protect your child. Try to pick a camping location with some shade so he or she can stay cool and out of the sun.

The sleeping bag. Believe it or not this actually can be a challenging issue. A baby can get lost in a regular child's sleeping bag (which also is heavy), but will need something to sleep in. I am sure there are baby sleeping bags on the market, but considering you may only use it a few times before the little one outgrows it, that may be an unneeded expense. Some parents who have sleeping bags that can zip together can put baby between them where he or she will sleep warm and cozy. Others develop some sort of contraption made of blankets that does not allow the little one to roll on out of the tent. Finally, if all else fails you can bring along a child's sleeping bag and just make sure your baby is dressed warmly in case he or she wiggles out of it. Synthetic bags are a good idea, because they wash up easier than down.

The Baby First Aid Kit is not the place to scrimp on weight. Don't forget to bring the diaper rash ointment, baby Tylenol or ibuprofen, baby sunscreen, baby wipes, antihistamine, and whatever else your kid may need.

When you arrive at your destination set up your camp first before unloading the little monster. It is probably best to have one person in charge of the child, while the other takes care of the initial camp chores. Once the tent is set up, if need be, you now have a prison, I mean playpen, to keep your bundle of joy in one place. Also, once your base camp is set up you can then take turns going on day hikes to enjoy a brief glimpse of bygone days. Or you can day-hike together carrying a much lighter load, because much of the weight is back in camp.

Now that you are done with the preliminaries, what is it really like backpacking with an infant? If you are an experienced backpacker, there are several other adjustments to get used to when traveling with infants and toddlers. You are an environmentally sensitive individual and understand the Leave No Trace rules of behavior. You have always kept a clean camp and taken great pains to not disturb your fellow campers by making too much noise. You walk softly and are careful not to destroy fragile plants. In other words, you are the kind of person who is good to the environment and is a joy to camp near. Once you bring along the infant, things change. Now you will be camping in crowded areas close to the trailhead, struggling to keep a clean camp while your infant is smearing food all over you, the dog, and himself. Then he gets up and stomps through the flowers before ripping out handfuls of the once-beautiful blooms, which are destined to be tossed summarily onto the ground. Instead of barely noticing that you are there, your backpacking neighbors may hear the sound of crying and screaming (and that's just you, wait until they hear the baby!). Hate to tell you this, but you might just have become that obnoxious camper across the lake that used to drive you nuts. Do your best to keep your kids quiet and try to save the flowers for the next family, but don't forget to give yourself a break. Try to teach them the right things, but remember that nobody is perfect. Be sure that they are having a good time and that if they remember the trip at all, it is a positive memory. Relax and enjoy the special sight of your two-year-old playing with the pollywogs, and when you pack up to leave, make sure no one can tell that you were ever there.

Dealing with rainstorms and hail is an interesting challenge for older children. With small children, on the other hand, you have to be willing to cancel the trip if the weather looks bad, or end it early before bad weather arrives. There is no sense endangering your child for a few days in the wilderness that they will never re-member anyway. Don't worry, you will have other opportunities.

While backpacking with infants certainly has its challenges, for most people the toughest age to deal with is between about 2½ and 7 years old. At this age they are too heavy to carry on your back (and they have no desire to be stuck up there anyway), and they are slow walkers and not capable of carrying a backpack. In addition, walking along narrow, steep trails can be dangerous for young children and scary for you. One option at this age is to carry in all your supplies on your back, while the child walks in unen-cumbered by any pack. In this scenario, you may only be able to go a mile or less, depending upon how good a little hiker you have, but once you get to the destination, you can take turns watching Junior, while your partner goes on day hikes.

Finally, remember this is your trip, too. I am reminded of the flight attendant's announcement, "Put your oxygen mask on your-self before putting it on the face of a small child." In your desire to make sure every need of your child is taken care of, it is easy to forget about yourself. Be sure to check your list so you have

Cooper decides it is time to get wet! Photo by Karen Honeywell

everything *you* need as well as what your child will need. It's great that you have your child's favorite blankee, but you also need to bring your sunglasses and medication. When you arrive at your destination don't forget to spend time nursing a hot chocolate and enjoying a few brief moments of quiet splendor on the shores of the lake. You deserve it. And the good news is that as your child gets older, it will get easier, and you will have introduced them to something that will stay with them forever.

CHAPTER 4

Having Fun and Being Safe

The best part about backpacking is when you get there
and you take off your backpack (finally!) and you see the
beautiful view. You go and search for the perfect spot to stay
(preferably close to the water) and just sit and relax for a little
while. I especially like rock-hopping across the lake, if you
can. It's really fun to make up a skit or a circus of unamazing
things, like standing on one foot while holding a bowl. I
especially like going exploring.

—Hannah Hauserman, 12

How to Enjoy Your Time
in the Wilderness

You have been reading up on everything you need to know about
backpacking with children. The packs have been checked and re-
checked, and you are wondering what you might have forgotten.
Before the rest of this chapter delves into safety and rules and all
that other necessary stuff, how about we take a deep breath and
focus on a few things that will make your trip fun.

    1. When you get to a lake or stream, the first thing you
need to do is jump in and splash the heck out of each
other. Lots of laughing and giggling is required. Then
get out, lie on a flat, smooth warm piece of rock and

don't say a word for 15 minutes as the water drips off and the sun warms you. Take nice long gentle breaths, gaze at the clouds and tell yourself, "Ah, now this is why I am here!"

2. Bring along a lightweight journal to commit all those awe-inspiring moments to memory. If you keep using the same journal, you can regale yourself and your hiking companions with stories about your past adventures. Be sure and write down the funny things your kids say, it will be great reading a few years down the road. Years ago my daughter was pretending to get married to her sister and solemnly recited the vows: "Do you take this woman for your awful life?" Now that is the kind of stuff you want to write down. The quiet hours on a backpack trip are also the perfect time to pull out that nature book by John Muir or Henry David Thoreau that you have always wanted to read. There is no time as relaxing as the quiet do-nothing time of a layover day on a backpacking trip.

3. Love and marvel at all that you see. The mountains have much beauty—smooth rock, tall green trees, crystal blue lakes, white patches of snow. The entire scene can bring such joy at the wonders of creation. A true appreciation of this beauty, and a desire to absorb it all, are the keys to successful backpacking. If the setting is extraordinary and takes your breath away, all the challenges and complications will be worth it. Spend the time to learn about the plants, the animals, the geology, etc., so you can fully appreciate what you are looking at.

4. Go to bed after looking at the stars, and get up early to watch the sunrise. Lie on a rock with your children and

gaze at the stars and the satellites until they ask you if they can go to sleep now. In the early morning, marvel at the wonderful light as the sun slowly marches across the neighboring mountains.

5. Try to consider any weather you run into on your trip as a win-win situation:

Hot and sunny—It's a beautiful day, enjoy the sunshine until it gets too hot, and then take a swim.

Raining—Enjoy the pitter-patter of raindrops, gaze through the mists, marvel at the water everywhere and the shine it gives the rocks and trees. After the heat of the sun, this pleasant cool-off makes everything look fresh and green.

Fog/low clouds—Appreciate the mystery as the layers of clouds and fog rise and lower with the winds.

Snow—It is so peaceful and quiet, it's as if the snow has absorbed all sound. Enjoy the whole new world of your winter wonderland.

Wind—The rustling and blowing through the trees makes a sound like a symphony, and the mosquitoes are blown away leaving you in the rarest of treats, a land without bugs.

Lightning—This is the one exception. If lightning threatens, it is best to retreat and head for safer ground.

The key to being able to appreciate all weather conditions is to have the right clothing and gear to meet any challenge or weather situation. If you are not too cold, or too warm, and both you and your gear are not wet, then you can enjoy whatever Mother Nature throws your way. It is a good idea to check the weather forecast before your trip and plan accordingly.

6. Get your child a hydration pack. After I kept turning around time after time to see one of my kids sucking away on my Camelback, I decided they needed hydration packs of their own. Kids really love having their own tube to suck away on. It's like a pacifier to help them through something new and different. Children (and adults) drink more water when they wear a hydration pack, which is a very good thing because it is easy for busy children to forget about drinking and get dehydrated. Another secret reason to give them a Camelback is that when the tube is in their mouth, they are walking instead of stopping, and when the tube is in their mouth, they can't whine that they are still walking.

7. Try to have patience with your children and your fellow hikers. If you are an experienced hiker it may be difficult to slow down and walk at kid speed. Yes, I admit it, it still does drive me crazy, but I am working on it. Remember, you are really not on a time schedule. Other than the time you have to be back home, you do not have to be anywhere at any time. Go with the flow and enjoy the little moments. When you want to scream that you have only gone ½ mile in the past hour, take a deep breath and look at the wildflowers or the snowfield. If hiking is slow and your children are complaining, try playing word games as you walk to distract them. One interesting game to play is to ask the children how many animals they can use as verbs. Examples include to steer, to fly, to pig out, to flounder, to perch, and, my favorite, to

Yippee! This is fun! Photo by Doug Greenwood

bee. Somebody with way too much time on their hands says there are at least 90 possibilities.

8. Play games, tell stories, be a kid.

9. Accept your backpacking experience for what it is: imperfect, limited, challenging, and unforgiving. But like the rest of life, very worth it.

Teach Your Children Well

Backpacking with children gives parents a marvelous opportunity to teach them without the kids even knowing they are being taught. After a number of backpack trips and hikes, my children have developed a good understanding of the common sense of nature. For example, they have learned that snow melts faster on a south-facing slope than a north-facing slope. This means you can hike on the south-facing slope earlier in the spring and the north-facing slope will have wildflowers still blooming late in the summer. They know that once you have set up camp, it is a good idea to walk around the area and explore. They will soon find that perfect flat rock for playing cards, the special spot for their morning bathroom duties, or the best location to eat and watch the sunset. My daughters and their hiking buddies have learned about snow tunnels, waterfalls, moths that are as big as hummingbirds, and eagles flying so high up in the sky you can barely see them. They have seen and heard coyotes and bears picking their way through rocks and understand what talus is. Contour maps and compasses, and, yes, even the names of trees and wildflowers are part of their repertoire. They have learned that as soon as the sun goes down it gets cold quickly and that the worst time for mosquitoes is just before dark. They know, without being told, that you need to keep a clean camp to keep away bears. While they can't recite all the principles, they certainly understand all the basic tenets of Leave No Trace and for the most part follow the rules.

What's great about teaching kids about nature and backpacking is that you learn it by doing it. It takes just a few trips and your children will become experts on tent design and sleeping pads. They will know their way around a backpacking stove and become champions at filtering water. Kids can wash two bowls, two cups, and two spoons with two drops of soap, and you all will be willing to eat off of those bowls when they are finished (the level of hygiene does tend to get a bit relaxed when on a backpacking trip).

What are the two most important things children learn?

1. That there are jobs to do. Whether it is setting up tents, making dinner, or filtering water it all has to be done before you can sleep or eat. So everybody needs to chip in and do their part. For some reason, it is much easier to get people to work together when there are no such

distractions as televisions, phones, or computers. In short order, the water is filtered, the tents are up; someone is digging into the canister for food, while someone else is bringing out cups and bowls. And after dinner one person is busy doing the dishes, while another is getting everything ready for bed. Not only are they learning how to work as a team, they are also learning about developing a work ethic. Pretty good for spending a few days a year out having fun in the wilderness.

2. If we teach them about the beauty of nature, and how it needs to be protected, they quickly appreciate it, and understand that our actions in the mountains directly affect the environment. My kids have a much deeper appreciation and love for nature since we began spending nights out under the stars. When the Sierra Club was formed over a hundred years ago, one of the first things they did was take people on overnight outings into the wilderness. The Club understood that when people spend time in the wilderness they begin to love it and want to make sure it is still there for their grandchildren to enjoy as well.

Once, on a field trip with my daughter to Mono Lake, I caught a presentation by Marshall Jack, a Native American medicine man. He said that as a child he was taught that our ancestors' blood is in our veins, and that we can feel our ancestors all around us when we are enjoying nature. He told us to always show our appreciation and thanks for all nature does for us, because in so doing we are honoring our ancestors. He said it was our responsibility to learn to live as part of nature, not as creatures who are separate from nature. The Native Americans believed that those who are not connected to nature are intent on conquering it. Unfortunately, the new arrivals from Europe believed that nature needed to be conquered (and they were interested in conquering the Native Americans as well, but that is another story).

When he was a child, Marshall told us, they would go to the river to fish. He was taught to move so slowly and quietly down to the edge of the river that the vibrations in his feet wouldn't alarm the fish. Then when he got to the edge of the stream, he was taught to move so slowly and carefully into it that he would become a part of the river. Then the fish would not consider him an alien creature, but just part of nature. With a hollow reed in his mouth for air, he would float so quietly and peacefully just below the surface of the river that he could tickle the belly of a fish or the feet of a duck, and they would not be afraid.

Will our children ever learn that level of appreciation for nature? Probably not, but if we help them learn to love nature and understand it we will be doing them, and the planet, a great service.

Should You Bring Rex?

Many children are in love with their dogs and can't imagine going on a backpacking trip without them. While most dogs will love the experience and relish the opportunity to jump into a lake or stream, some smaller breeds may not be suited to backpacking. If you have an outdoorsy dog that you frequently take hiking, it may be a good candidate.

Your first step is to pick up a doggie backpack. Go on the Internet or to your local dog supply retailer, and you should be able to find a good one. The rule is that dogs can safely carry about ⅓ of their body weight. Unless it is a real long trip, this should include all of their food and perhaps a few other things. The good news is that when you are hiking out, most of their food will be gone, and they can carry some garbage and other items that will reduce your weight and get those dirty diapers and smelly stuff out of your

Dogs love to camp, and we love them carrying our garbage. Photo by Doug Greenwood

pack (and we all know dogs like smelly stuff). Be sure their food is safely ensconced in a plastic bag, because dogs will be running into the water with their packs on.

Once you have a doggie pack, before heading out overnight put it on your dog and take it on a few walks so it gets used to it. Make sure your dog's paws have been toughened up for a long trip on rocky trails, and just in case, you may want to bring along a set of dog booties.

Once your dog is ready, determine whether dogs are allowed where you want to camp (and if they are not, don't go there! When people take their dogs where they are not supposed to, it just makes officials more likely to want to prohibit dogs throughout their purview). Dogs are prohibited on national park and national monument trails, and in many wilderness areas. They are not permitted in many state parks as well. The good news is there are areas that allow dogs. Contact your local public land officials to find the best places to go. Be sure that the area you will be hiking will have plenty of water for Fido to drink, and make the effort to stop at water sources so your dog will take the time to drink. On a hot day, try to get Rex into the water to cool off.

Once you are on the trail, you need to keep your dog under control. If it cannot resist growling at fellow hikers, or chasing that deer or porcupine that strolls on by, then it needs to be on a leash. In addition, many people go to the wilderness to find peace and quiet. Keep your dog from barking, especially at night, when other people are trying to sleep. It is your responsibility as well to bury the dog's waste, whether it is on or off the trail. Some truly responsible individuals now carry dog waste back out. Remember, dog food, like any other food or smelly object, needs to go into a bear canister at night.

If you decide to bring the dog, you need to be prepared for a few eventualities. If it rains you may need to bring that muddy, smelly creature into the tent with you. Check your dog on a regular basis for ticks and burrs, and try to keep it out of foxtails and poison oak or ivy, or you may be the one paying the price in itching or veterinarian bills. Bring along a little first aid kit for the dog with antibiotic ointment and some wrap designed for dog bandages. Just in case all of your best intentions are for naught, and Fifi just can't stay away from that lovely little porcupine, you may want to bring along a pair of needle-nose pliers for quill removal. Finally, be sure to keep your dog securely in your tent or leashed at night. A friend of mine tells a story about how her dog wandered off in the night and then came tearing back full speed with her tail between her legs, with a mountain lion following close behind.

Overcoming Fears

An important part of backpacking is learning how to overcome your fears. As an adult it is important that you get past your fears, so that you can deal with the ones your children may be confronting. If you are not familiar with spending the night in the wilderness it can be pretty frightening. And for some of us, even after a lot of time in the woods, it can be scary. The best way to overcome fears is to be prepared, but not frightened. There is nothing quite like backpacking to bring out fears that you didn't even know you had. So what fears do backpackers confront? One biggie for me is the fear of heights, as in walking along cliff edges. Then there is the fear of being eaten or mauled by a bear or mountain lion, which is a common fear for many. How about breaking a leg, catching on fire, or starving to death? If it is cold enough, you could also freeze to death. Finally, you could have a heart attack or appendicitis out in the middle of nowhere where no one can help you. Those are the big fears. All are extremely unlikely to happen, and most are preventable. In fact, the most dangerous part of backpacking for many is leaving the house and driving to the trailhead.

I believe we are all victims of media sensationalism. It is the big or dramatic event that attracts our attention and brings about fear. We hear about the rare animal attack or lightning strike and focus on that instead of the reality, which is that millions and millions of hikers and backpackers go out every year without incident. There is a certain level of risk in all activities, and if you just sit around on your posterior you will face other dangers, like obesity, heart disease, diabetes, and cancer.

Overcoming fears is one of the great accomplishments of backpacking. The more time you spend in the wilderness the easier it should be to deal with the big fears. Just keep on hiking and you will get through it, and when you do you can congratulate yourself for a job well done. The more you can face down what scares you in the woods, the better you will be at dealing with the day-to-day stuff you encounter in your life.

Aside from the big fears, backpackers confront little fears as well. What if my stove doesn't work? What if all my clothes get wet? What if my sleeping pad gets a hole in it? Thinking about (but not obsessing on) these little fears while you are preparing for the trip will make your adventure more successful. Double-check the stove at home to make sure it works. Bring along waterproof clothes and several big plastic garbage bags to keep things dry. Be sure to pack repair kits for the sleeping pad and tent. Go over your list several times to make sure you have everything you may need in case of an emergency. If you know you are well prepared, it will put you at ease during your trip.

Forget About the Lions and Tigers, What About Those Bears?

Bear stories. Anyone who has lived in bear country for more than a few years has some good ones to tell. Whether they are breaking into cars, wandering through vacant homes, or stealing food hanging from trees, bears are running into humans more and more frequently. My encounters with bears have invariably been interesting, sometimes downright frightening, and always awe-inspiring.

My first exposure to bears was on a backpacking trip to Yosemite when I was in high school. We were a group of seven friends camping near Half Dome. We followed the bear-proof procedures popular in the 1970s—we placed our food in a bag tied between two trees high up in the air and crossed our fingers. I remember a bear up one tree trying to reach the bag, while Greg Jones (later to win a medal in skiing in the 1976 Olympics) was up in the other tree trying to grab the bag before the bear got it. Those of us on the ground were attempting to scare the bear away by throwing sticks and rocks at it. The bear, pretty much oblivious to our petty efforts, eventually got a portion of our food and dragged it off into the woods. Greg chased the bear, which then turned and charged him. Fortunately for America's future Olympic hopes, the bear stopped short before reaching Greg and waddled off to find its next victim.

When I moved to the edge of the National Forest on the west

shore of Lake Tahoe in the late 1980s, I began to have regular encounters with bears. One early morning, I was staring out the window bleary-eyed when I noticed a big cinnamon-colored bear with his entire mouth wrapped around my daughter's plastic swing. It was a mouth that looked like it could chomp down on a garbage can without much fuss. On another occasion, I awoke to the sound of a bear ripping apart a stump next to the master bedroom. Several times while watching TV in the family room I have looked out the window to see a bear about three feet away (perhaps it was watching TV as well; bears hate the commercials, except for that one where a bear walks into a grocery store and, after showing his ID, is allowed to purchase beer). It is amazing how big bears appear when they are standing on two feet and looking into your window. Our ultimate bear story began, not with a bear, but a bat. A bat was flying around in our living room and, as we had been advised, at dusk we set about the task of removing it. As we flailed ineffectively at the bat with a broom in an effort to get it to fly out the open back door, I heard a noise on the other side of the house. As I rushed in to the family room, a bear was poking his nose through the window screen, trying to get closer to the smell of our salmon dinner.

Every year, the third-grade class from Tahoe Lake Elementary School and many of the parents go camping at D. L. Bliss State Park on the west shore of Lake Tahoe. I volunteered to be one of the camp guards for the evening for my daughter's class. In the middle of the night, I heard a noise and discovered a bear attempting to break his way into a Subaru packed with camp food. As he calmly ripped the trim off the car, several parents were trying to decide how we could get the bear and his buddy to leave without waking up a group of 50 third-graders. Our tepid effort revolved around shining flashlights at him and softly saying, "Go bear . . . go away, bear." We might even have said please. The bear eventually lumbered off, only to return a few hours later. Perhaps we should have let the kids wake up. Fifty screaming third-graders would have kept bears away from the campground for weeks.

My scariest bear story happened in the middle of a hot early-summer day, only 200 yards from the Meeks Bay trailhead at Lake Tahoe. I was returning from a great hike to Crag Lake and was daydreaming my way back to the car when I noticed an enormous bear cross the dirt road about 50 yards in front of me. I stopped and with my jaw dropping, watched the next one, who was even bigger. Soon they were splashing around in the creek, about 100 yards away. After carefully watching and listening to them for a minute, I started walking again on the trail. I heard some loud splashing and looked to see the bigger of the two bears charging me at full speed. To me, he was a fast-moving, splashing behemoth on his way to devour me and within what felt like a second he was about 30 yards away. It felt like one of those nature movies with the grizzly bear running toward the camera. Just so you know, they can run really, really fast. Somehow I remembered not to run and just got angry. I spread my legs out, threw my arms into the air and yelled as loud as I could: "Heyyyyyy!!!! I'm standing here!!!" The bear stopped in his tracks, turned around and went to play with his mate. I pooped in my pants, fainted, and then, after regaining consciousness, slowly walked out while the rush of adrenaline hit my head. That evening, still trying to relax from my adventure, I turned on the TV and began flipping through the channels. I came to a horror movie with a big nasty bear growling and making a bloody mess of some poor guy's face. Sleep tight.

Violent black bear encounters are very rare, and usually it is a mistake by a human that causes them to happen. Black bears in general try to avoid confrontation, and as long as they consider you the king of the forest they will back off. As humans continue to invade bear habitat and provide free meals for bears, human-bear encounters are sure to increase. Hikers need to make sure bears do not have access to human food. A common refrain in

What to Do If You See a Bear

If you see a black bear be sure to do the following:

1. If the bear is in your territory, which includes your house, tent, backpack, or car, attempt to scare it away by making lots of noise, shouting at it, and throwing your arms around. Be sure not to block the bear's exit, and remember that it will always leave the same way it came in.

2. If you come around a corner and startle a bear, you are now in its territory. Back away slowly and give the bear a chance to amble off into the forest. Talk to it gently but firmly to let it know you are human.

3. If the bear has stolen your food, don't try to take it back! Once he has your food, you are not going to get it back! And with bear slobber all over it, do you really want it back?

4. Never get between a mother bear and her cub. While I have heard this rule of bear behavior for many years, some bear experts now feel that the danger has been exaggerated. To approach cubs no matter where they are is dangerous. Especially for your pride, when your friends call you an idiot and say, "What were you thinking"?

Grizzly bears only reside in a few places in the United States, and they behave differently than black bears. While they also usually avoid human confrontation, they do consider themselves a little higher on the food chain than black bears, and have been known to attack humans. If you are hiking in grizzly country, you should contact the local forest personnel for information on rules, regulations, and suggestions. The old joke about the difference between black bears and grizzlies is that black bears will climb the tree to get to you, while the grizzly will just knock the tree down.

I highly recommend the use of bear canisters to reduce bear encounters. It is important for the survival of the bear, and to prevent you from having to hike out hungry, that you make sure they don't have access to your food. Your bear container must not only contain all of your food, but anything else that has a scent to it, such as toothpaste or sunscreen.

Since bears are all about smell, long-distance hikers have discovered that one way to avoid bear confrontations is not to sleep where you cook. Take a break to create a smelly dinner while en route to your destination and then hike a few more miles to your camping spot.

An excellent source for information on bears is the Bear League located at Lake Tahoe. They can be reached at www.savebears.org or (530) 525-PAWS.

mountain communities is: "A fed bear is a dead bear." Once bears are habituated to humans they may keep coming back until they become dangerous and end up having to be killed.

In the Interest of Safety

Most emergency situations are avoided by planning ahead and using that mass of tissue between your ears. It is much easier to avoid an emergency than to get out of one. The first step to planning ahead is to take a wilderness first aid class. To show that you are really smart, have your hiking buddies do so as well—so they can save you. A detailed analysis of first aid is beyond the scope of this book, but a few of the most important first aid issues you will encounter in backcountry travel include: dehydration, hypothermia, sunburn, frostbite, broken bones and sprains, abrasions, insect bites, burns, choking, altitude sickness, and the most common—blisters and other foot problems. While it is recommended you take the class to learn how to cure these maladies, almost all of these potential trip killers are preventable. Here are a few suggestions:

> **Dehydration/heat exhaustion/sunstroke**—Remind yourself and your child to drink fluids on a regular basis and try to stay out of the hot sun. Drink more than you think you will need. If it is hot, wear light-colored clothing and less of it. If you or your children start exhibiting signs of heat exhaustion (paleness, dizziness, nausea, fainting, and increased temperature), stop, get into the shade immediately, and drink fluids that contain electrolytes. Wait to continue your hike until you feel better.

> **Hypothermia**—When it is cold, stay out of the water and bring appropriate clothing layers. If you get wet, stay out of the wind and get yourself to a warm place where you can remove the wet clothes.

Sunburn—Remind your child to wear sunscreen and apply it regularly. Wear a hat. Try to limit your sun exposure in camp by spending time in the shade.

Frostbite—Protect your extremities from ice and water. Bring gloves if you are traveling into areas that will be cold. As with hypothermia, if you get cold and wet, find a warm place and change into dry clothes.

Broken bones/sprains/abrasions—Be careful out there. Tell your little hiking buddies to have fun but to not be too reckless. If the kids are running around camp, make sure they have on good shoes for running. Use hiking poles and appropriate footwear.

Insect bites—Remember, early morning and just before dark are the worst times for mosquitoes. Wear repellent, stay out of marshy areas, find rocky areas with a breeze, and wear long pants and long shirts when mosquitoes are active. If you or your child is allergic to bees, be sure and bring along antihistamines and/or an epinephrine pen. With West Nile virus and other mosquito-borne diseases becoming more common in the United States, it has become more important than ever to keep from getting bitten by mosquitoes.

Choking—Relax, breathe, and take the time to chew slowly. If your child has the giggles, tell him to stop eating until they subside and to save the really funny joke for after dinner. If while he's laughing liquids are emerging from his nose, that is a sign that eating should not continue until after the laughter settles down. Choking is especially dangerous to the lone hiker. Be extra careful when you are hiking alone to chew your food thoroughly.

Altitude sickness—If you are unaccustomed to the high altitude, try to spend a few days near the trailhead before beginning your trek. Go slowly the first day or two, and if you find you or your child has symptoms of altitude sickness (dizzy, difficulty breathing, headaches, nausea) treat it accordingly. A mild case may be cured by taking a break to give yourself a chance to acclimate. If it is more serious you may have to descend to a lower elevation. For most people, it is amazing the difference a thousand feet of descent can make. I remember once feeling pretty horrible at the top of Mt. Whitney (14,494 feet). I was dizzy, had a stomachache, headache, and no appetite. By the time I descended to 12,000 feet I felt like I was on top of the world—hungry, happy, and ready to go.

Foot problems—You are carrying about 40 extra pounds and walking miles over rough terrain, and you are surprised your feet hurt? Take care of your feet by taking regular breaks and putting your toes in some cold water. Keep your doggies clean, and if you have the hint of a hot spot or blister treat it right away (duct tape of course is one possibility. If that doesn't work you can always use Windex, because as we all know from the movies, Windex is good for everything).

Before you set out on the trail, tell someone *where* you are going, *when* you expect to be back (give yourself some extra time so everybody is not freaked out if you are a little late), and *who* you are going with. It is best if the someone you tell where you are going can hike and is familiar with the area where you are hiking. Perhaps you could leave them a map clearly indicating your planned route. Knowledge of the area can be a real asset when it comes time to give information to rescue personnel. Remember to let your contact person know when you have safely returned to the trailhead so they don't start a search effort.

On the trail, bring a guidebook, a map, and a compass, and know how to use them. Topographic maps are good tools to teach children about nature and landforms. On these maps, also known as contour maps, lines represent contours or elevations. The closer together the lines are the steeper the elevation gains and losses are on the ground. If you spend time looking at maps as you are hiking or in camp, your children will develop an understanding of map reading. They will soon be able to recognize how steep a hike they will be making the next day, or where a cliff is located on the map. While being able to read maps is important from a safety point of view, as your map-reading skills improve it also opens up a new world of possible places to hike. Now armed with a map you can walk off-trail, follow ridgelines, avoid steep hills or cliffs, and make your way to some isolated lake that is not accessible by trail. Map reading or orienteering classes are taught throughout the country so keep your eyes open for one near you.

It is a good idea to keep referring to your map as you are hiking along so you always know where you are. Familiarize yourself with what the nearby landforms are at all times, because when an emergency happens, you may be too flustered to spend a lot of time looking at maps trying to determine your location. If you have been mentally keeping track then you will know, "OK, I just passed Big Rock Candy Mountain, so that lake down there must be Whatchamadingle Lake." Based on that information you can make an informed decision about what to do next.

While I believe it is usually a good experience for older children to do a little exploring, they should be in sight or shouting range of you at all times. If possible, they should do their exploring with a friend. Tell them while they are walking to keep track of where they are and notice landmarks like a pile of rocks, an interesting tree, or a pretty meadow. Children should carry a whistle

Hey, Dad! Let's go for a ride. Photo by Karen Honeywell

with them that should be used if they are lost (and only if they are lost). Tell them that if they feel confused and are not sure where they are, they should follow the instructions frequently given by search-and-rescue groups: STOP—Stop, Think, Observe, Plan. Then if necessary they should blow the whistle until you arrive. In order to keep your children from getting scared, be sure to let them know before you leave on your trip that while getting lost is a concern, it is rare and as long as they follow the few simple precautions outlined above they should be fine.

Plan for all types of weather and understand the weather conditions in your area. Start by keeping a close eye on the weather forecast before your trip, but understand that sometimes forecasts are wrong. If it is midsummer and you are in an area that is susceptible to lots of thunderstorms, try to get off the top of exposed mountains or ridges before the middle of the afternoon. The best place to be during a thunderstorm (aside from the inside of your home or car) is in the middle of a clump of smaller trees in a forest. If the storm is very close, try to stay away from metal objects such as hiking poles, backpacks, etc., and open bodies of water, such as lakes or ponds. If you are caught in the open, try to stay low and crouch down or sit on your backpack (unless it contains a lot of metal). Remember that your children might be more scared of thunder and lightning than you are, so when you reach a safe spot, do your best to comfort them.

Make sure your tent site is safe. Any dead trees hanging over your tent? Is there a high danger of lightning in this location? Are you at the bottom of a talus field with rocks tumbling down around you? Is this a dry streambed waiting for that thunderstorm to turn it into a raging torrent? Or a game trail that Brother Bear will be walking by on any minute? Is it time to move your tent somewhere safer?

Are you in an area with ticks? If so, be sure to check your children regularly. Whether it is from wandering on- and off-trail through the bushes, or playing games in the forest, kids are vulnerable to picking up ticks. If the tick has not settled in yet, just brush it off. Once it is lodged in the skin, you need to remove the tick carefully with a tick-removing tool (tweezers) that are in most wilderness first aid kits. If you are traveling in an area prone to Lyme disease, you need to pack out the tick so that it can be checked for Lyme disease by health service personnel when you return to civilization.

Speaking of wandering off-trail, if you are in an area that has lots of poison oak or ivy, make sure your little ones understand what it looks like and instruct them to keep away. Ivy Block helps to prevent a reaction to poisonous plants. It is probably a good idea to rub it on if you are in an area where your children are likely to encounter poison oak or ivy. If you encounter stinging nettles, good luck, those things really hurt. So try to avoid them. Often guidebooks will inform you whether nettles or poison oak may be present along a particular trail.

An important precaution for spending time near water is to make sure that your children have learned to swim. I would highly recommend that kids get swimming lessons as early as possible. Learning how to swim is not only for the children's protection, but your kids will have a blast swimming in a mountain lake or playing in a cool stream. If your children, however, have not learned to swim, be especially watchful and keep an eye on them at all times when they are next to a body of water. If you have non-swimmers, it is probably best to camp far enough away from water so that they cannot quickly wander into trouble.

Stream crossings, especially in the spring when mountain snowmelt is at its swiftest, can be treacherous. When you are planning your trip, attempt to determine if there may be difficult crossings along the route (guidebooks describing the route will often provide details on potentially wet fords). If you know there may be a difficult crossing, try to get there earlier in the morning. As daytime temperatures rise, melting snows raise the level of rivers and streams. If your planning fails you, however, and you reach a stream with water running too fast and deep to cross, first try to find an alternative route. Put down your pack and scout upstream and down looking for a good location to cross. Is there a large downed log nearby? A line of big rocks sticking out of the water? Often the best place to cross may be where the stream becomes wider and shallower. If the water is not too deep, you can take off your boots and put on your sport sandals or water socks to make the crossing. If the water looks too swift or deep for you to find an alternative way across, evaluate closely the river for the best location to cross, use a hiking stick or piece of wood, and cross with caution. If there is any question whether the stream can be crossed easily by children, adults should go into the stream first. Several different methods can be used to cross: If you have a group of four or more people, you can hold hands and slowly walk across together. A group of three may want to all hold hands together and cross sideways. With a parent and child, it might be best to have the parent upstream and the child downstream, with each putting their hands on the other's shoulders. Unstrap your hip belt and sternum strap before going into deeper water, so that if you fall you can quickly get out of your pack. Another option is to use a rope to get across. Designate the first person to carry the rope as he or she crosses, and then set up a crossing line that children can hold on to as they go over to the other side. Make sure they are downstream of the rope. Finally, if you determine that the river is just too dangerous to cross, you may have to abort your trip or change the itinerary to cross at a different location.

Aside from streams, nice calm lakes can also be hazardous. The biggest danger for older children is that in the midst of chasing each other around rocks and over logs they may trip and hit their head on a rock before going into the water. Tell your children to exercise caution, and monitor them to make sure that games don't get out of hand—but remember they are supposed to be exploring and having fun, so don't be too paranoid. Just be extra vigilant when your children are close to water.

In the Sierra Nevada, as well as many other mountainous locations, snowpack in some locations can last into the summer. Usually during the spring the snowpack is firm in the morning and softer in the afternoon, making for pleasurable morning hikes and wet shoes in the afternoon. Hiking over snow on a flat trail is usually just refreshing, but a steep snow-covered traverse can be treacherous. Sometimes it is safer to walk around the snow patch or follow a pattern of footprints across the snow. Walking sticks can be helpful for traversing across a snowy slope. Watch for hollow areas where a tunnel has formed under the snow; these can collapse when you walk over them. Check with the local rangers or park personnel to determine whether the trail you will be hiking is snow free. I would certainly not recommend aborting a trip because the ranger tells you there are a few patches of snow on the trail, but if the word is that 90 percent of the trail is snow covered, you may want to find another destination.

But enough about all the warnings and safety, time for another quick fun break. Snow can also be really fun on the trail. You can slide down it or have a snowball fight. You can lie down in it to cool off on a hot day. Sometimes melting snow forms beautiful tunnels over fast-moving streams, or soft blue icebergs floating in mountain lakes. Don't miss the bliss.

If you travel off-trail you may encounter fields of boulders or talus. These are areas where you will walk some distance, stepping from rock to rock. I think of boulders as larger, more stable rocks, while talus is numerous foot-sized or slightly larger rocks all clumped together in a large pile. For boulders, you need to walk carefully from rock to rock, to have stable footing. While they often make for slow hiking, most boulder fields are fairly safe. Talus is more treacherous, as the rocks tend to move around as you walk. Talus is one of the most frustrating places to walk, because it is hard to establish surefootedness, and you always have the feeling that the rock will give out under you. Try to step on the uphill side of the rocks, which should make them less likely to slip. When possible, limit the distance you walk between boulders or talus fields, because they are not only dangerous, but it can also be very time consuming. It takes much longer to walk over a field of talus than it does to walk on dirt, so keep that in mind when "shortcutting" via a rock field. I remember walking through a large field of talus on a section of the Tahoe Rim Trail that was still under construction. We followed the markers where the trail was scheduled to be built, and it took us about an hour to stumble and swear our way across the difficult terrain on the shoulder of Rose Knob Peak. A year later, on the now-completed section of trail built through the rock field, I strolled through the same area in about five minutes.

One more safety tip: Get yourself in shape. Many of the problems encountered in the backcountry occur because people are not physically prepared for the challenges of backpacking. If you do not exercise much, and your idea of a workout is to use the television remote or walk to the refrigerator to get a piece of pie and a beer, you should check with your doctor before embarking on a major trip.

Keep in the back of your mind, especially when hiking with children, that safety comes first. Even if it means turning around before it gets dark or when a thunderstorm is approaching. Everyone knows this, but in the heat of the moment it is easy to make mistakes and travel when you shouldn't. Accidents can happen to anyone, but it is important to make decisions that are less likely to lead to an accident.

In spite of all your careful planning, you may need to initiate an evacuation of a member of your party. Once, I was in a group of six people who carried a woman in a litter about ¼ mile on a hiking trail. It was a gentle downhill, but we were all exhausted by the time we reached our destination. I was astounded by how difficult it was. Are those glum looks you see on pallbearers sadness for the dearly departed or just grimaces from all the weight? If it's necessary to evacuate someone, if at all possible, help them to walk out. Victims can walk out with a broken arm and sprains and strains on their legs. If you have to carry someone out it will take a lot of people, a lot of time, and a lot of energy. If you have to evacuate from a long distance, and you only have a few people, the victim may be better served by someone (or several people, depending upon how many are in your group) swiftly exiting to get help.

Finally, it is important to understand the group you are with. Does anybody have any allergies? Problems with altitude? Is anyone prone to illness? These are important factors to consider before embarking on your trip. An allergy to bees or other insects can sometimes be life-threatening. You should be informed and act accordingly.

Oh, and by the way, never forget the most important thing: Have fun. It is my job to make sure you are aware of all the safety issues, but the vast majority of backpackers return safely after having encountered no safety concerns. Plan ahead and use your head and you will be fine.

Water

There are people who have successfully drunk untreated water many times without getting sick. There are also lots of people who have consumed water that they thought was safe and have come down with a case of *Giardia*. To me, it is not worth the risk, so to avoid Rectal Dysfunction NEVER drink the water when you are on a backpacking trip until after you have filtered it, boiled it, or treated it with iodine. All three methods have advantages and disadvantages:

> **Filtered**—Filtering is easy and quick, and removes most of the bugs and debris out of your water. It also gives you cool, good tasting water. On the downside, filters are extra weight, will require an initial investment and sometimes have mechanical failures. While very effective, they are not 100 percent guaranteed to remove everything that might hurt you.

Boiled—If you boil your water supply before using it, you don't have to bring along a water filter, and boiling kills almost everything that could harm you. In fact, some bugs, like *Giardia,* are actually killed with hot water below the boiling point, but to be safe, boil it. Most experts say you just need to bring the water to a boil, others say it should boil for several minutes. Boiling, however, is a hassle. You have to take the time and have the fuel to boil water, and then you have to wait for it to cool before drinking. To boil all the water you will need in camp for eating and cleaning can be very time-consuming. Some hikers filter water to drink, but boil the water that they use to cook and clean.

Iodine (Chemical)—Chemicals are very lightweight, inexpensive, and not susceptible to mechanical failure. On the downside, you have to wait for the iodine to work, it tastes bad (although after treatment you can add pills containing vitamin c or powder drinks like Tang or Gatorade to make it taste better), and, as with boiling water, it is a trick to keep little twigs, bugs, and dirt from getting into the water.

In summary, when you're traveling with children my recommendation would be to filter water. If you are on your own and wish to travel light, chemicals are certainly a good alternative. Since water filters sometimes die on a trip, I always bring along chemical treatment tablets as well. Whatever method you use, the key is to drink lots of water, and make sure your kids do as well. Dehydration can be a serious problem with children, and they are often too busy to think about drinking. If your child gets a headache on a backpacking trip, suspect dehydration and treat it accordingly. Bring along water bottles for filtering water in camp. I find that I

Smile, you're at Lake Aloha.

drink more water while hiking if I use a hydration system on the trail.

Check your map frequently as you hike so you are aware of where you can find water over the next few miles. If you are running low on water, be careful not to pass the only source for the next 10 miles. If you are hiking in the late summer or fall, especially if you are in the Sierra or other areas that see little rain in the summer, be aware that many small streams or creeks will dry up by late summer.

Rules, Regulations, and Good Behavior

Fortunately, most of America would rather sit on the couch and watch TV than go backpacking. That leaves more room in the woods for those of us who are smart enough to hit the trail. That said, it can still be pretty crowded in the wilderness, and our actions can have a lasting negative impact on the environment. As stated earlier, it is your responsibility to teach your children to walk softly, love what they see, and leave it as they found it. A set of principles, known as Leave No Trace, has been developed to help hikers and campers use the backcountry without destroying it or negatively impacting other campers. Based on these principles, and a few of my own experiences, I have developed my set of rules.

Top Ten Ways to Be Good in the Woods

1. Camp at least 200 feet away from any water source. If there are already developed campsites closer to the water, and camping farther away would mean creating a new campsite in a pristine area, then it may be a better idea to camp in the existing campsite. When it comes time to do #2, however, that has to be done at least 200 feet away from a water source—the farther away the better. Remember, you drink and swim in this water.

2. Keep your mouth shut and your eyes open. One of my biggest bugaboos when I am out backpacking is that loud family across the way who feels like the best thing to do in the wilderness is make lots of noise. For many people, the best part about wilderness is that you can find the rarest of all commodities: quiet. Quiet enough that you can actually hear the sound of wind rushing through trees or water cascading down rocks. If you want to wreck the quiet with an iPod that is up to you, but keep the noise to yourself. I also understand that a little leeway needs to be given to the backpacker who has hauled in an infant or younger child, but if your

Boys marching along in the Tahoe National Forest. Photo by Doug Greenwood

children are big enough to understand the concept, let's try to keep 'em quiet.

3. Use cell phones only for emergencies. Those of us who go to the wilderness to escape from phones don't really need or want the reminder of reality. Use this opportunity to escape from the phone yourself; you might actually discover it is pretty cool to be without it for a few days. Who knows, when you return to civilization, you may discover you can actually go days at a time without using your cell phone. Anyone who conducts business in front of other individuals via cell phone in the wilderness should be summarily tossed into the closest body of water. Upon exiting from the lake, they must promise to leave the cell phone off for the duration of the trip.

4. It is hard to believe it is even necessary to make this statement, but don't smoke in the woods. The danger of fire is often extreme, and what are you going to do with those yecky butts? Not to mention that it is disgusting and will kill you.

5. If it doesn't grow there, it doesn't go there—banana peels, peach pits, apple cores, orange peels. If you take it in, take it out. Whatever it is. All of it.

6. Don't wash your dishes, or yourself, with soap in a lake or stream. Take your water at least 200 feet from the lake, and wash dishes on a nice flat rock (a good clean place for air-drying), then dump the water into the bushes. Remember, if you pack it in, pack it out, so any food waste should be packed out. Plan ahead to make sure you can eat all the food you cook. When you are finished with your meal in the backcountry, if you still have a few food scraps, filter them out with a pair of pantyhose (preferably old used ones) or cheesecloth. Rinse out your pot or bowl into the pantyhose. The water comes out, but the food scraps stay in, then bring it all out with the rest of your garbage.

7. Keep a clean campsite. Don't leave any pieces of food hanging around to attract bears, marmots, squirrels, birds, or other creatures. Once animals have discovered that this is a place to find food, they will come back for more the next time they see someone camping in the same spot. And remember, a fed bear is a dead bear. A fed squirrel, on the other hand, becomes an obnoxious beggar the next time someone camps in the same spot. When you reach the top of Mt. Tallac near Lake Tahoe it is best to enjoy the beautiful view and then find another place to have your lunch. So many people have fed the squirrels over the years that to protect your food you will have to fight them off with rocks.

8. Practice good trail-hiking etiquette. Remember when you are hiking on the trail: lead, follow, or get out of the way. In other words, if you are hiking along and a faster hiker overtakes you, move aside and let hm/her pass. Be sure your children are aware of this rule as well. To avoid erosion and the creation of new trails, stay on the trail and don't take shortcuts. If you are taking a break, move well off the trail so other hikers can easily pass. If you encounter horses on the trail, move off the trail to the downhill side and speak to the rider. This allows the horse to understand that you are human and not to be feared. If you are traveling off-trail, spread your group out so you do not create a new trail. As much as possible, walk on rock and other durable surfaces.

9. Carry out environmentally sensitive pooping and peeing.

> **Pooping in the woods**—You gotta do it, and you gotta do it right. There is a whole book on the subject, but my children will not allow me to mention the title here (you can find it in the reference list at the end of this book). Follow several rules:
>
> > Do your duties at least 200 feet from any body of water or trail.
> >
> > If possible, find a place with dark, organic topsoil. I also like a spot with some rocks to place my hands for leverage and a nice view, but sometimes we can't be too picky. Try to take your time finding the great spot and

enjoy the experience of wandering around in the woods.

Dig a cathole, hopefully about six inches deep, and four to six inches in diameter. After you're finished, use a stick to mix it all up, then cover it up with dirt and disguise it with natural materials (you will never think of the word "it" in the same way again).

Pack out used toilet paper and feminine hygiene products in plastic bags with baking soda, cat litter, or lime. If you need additional privacy, you can wrap the items in duct tape, and place them in a dark plastic bag (then wrap them in five more layers of plastic, put on a mask, and rubber gloves). Make sure you are aware of local regulations. Some heavily used, fragile areas now require you to remove all of your waste (sounds like enough of a reason to avoid those areas).

Peeing in the woods—Urine is sterile, but the salt in urine can hurt plants, so pee on rocks, bare dirt, or pine duff, not in your cathole or on the plants. To spread the impact, try to pee your initials on the ground. I understand this may be a little easier for the guys than girls. The letter T is easy, but I imagine "s" or "Q" could be a bit hard for a girl.

If you are new to this peeing in the wilderness thing it can be a bit tricky. Try not to pee on your pants or shoes, ladies. Sometimes if you find a very private spot it is easier just to take your pants all the way off and lay them aside (uphill and far enough away so that you are not helplessly watching as your stream of fluid quickly drains down to your pants). A lady friend of mine had several other recommendations for women peeing in the woods: Squat really low. Find a spot that puts your feet above the peeing spot. Hug a tree and lean way back.

When finished pooping or peeing, make sure you are well away from any sources of water, and wash your hands!

10. Leave everything where it is, and how it is, so the next person can enjoy it too. This means that you should not carve "Debbie loves Dopie" on an aspen tree. It also means that you should leave bird feathers, rocks, plants, or animals where they lie. The one thing you don't have to leave is garbage that you find in the woods. Make the extra effort for the environment by picking it up and packing it out. You can help the next hiker experience the joy of not seeing someone else's garbage.

LEAVE NO TRACE PRINCIPLES

The Leave No Trace principles have been devised to help people simply understand environmental ethics. Remember, ethics are not rules and regulations, but what you do when nobody is watching.

Leave No Trace principles were developed by the Leave No Trace Center for Outdoor Ethics, which can be reached at www.lnt.org. They have a number of programs designed to increase awareness of the importance of Leave No Trace principles, including PEAK (Promoting Environmental Awareness in Kids), sponsored by REI. PEAK educates children about responsible use of the outdoors.

Twenty Quick Tips for
Backpacking with Kids

Do you need a little more information and some quick ideas on how to make your backpacking trip more enjoyable? Remember . . .

1. Don't go too far, take it slowly, enjoy the journey, and whenever possible make sure to visit a lake or creek at the end.

2. Explore, play, have fun—how far and where you go are secondary. It is being together and enjoying nature that your children will remember. If you are looking for the major workout or to set personal distance records, wait until you go by yourself.

3. Sometimes it is the little things that can mess up a trip, so make sure everyone puts on sunscreen and reapplies it on a regular basis. Then be sure to keep children fed and hydrated. You probably won't have to remind them to eat, but you may have to remind them to drink.

4. Keep talking or play games while hiking to distract children from their potential misery. It might work on the parent as well. For many children it is the walking part that is the most difficult, so try to help them to focus on something else.

5. Bring cards and a good lightweight paperback for a rainy day in the tent. Looking for something good to read? Go to the appendix for some suggestions.

6. Quit the lesson while it is still fun. This is not a class, just have fun and live it and they will learn.

7. Take a layover day at a nice lake. This is the highlight of

You should see my funny face.

the trip for most kids. Hours of swimming make up for hours of hiking.

8. Bring a friend. Your children love you, but they may have more fun with their friend.

9. Learn enough about backpacking and hiking to feel comfortable in the woods. Go on lots of day hikes first and then go on a short one- or two-night overnight to apply what you have learned. Take several years to build up to a longer trip with your child.

10. Don't be discouraged after a tough sleepless night or when you can't get things to work. It will work out, and even if it doesn't you will survive (most likely). Focus on the joy.

11. Love the ones you're with, or at least learn from them. Watch experienced backpackers and copy them. It is OK to steal ideas from other hikers—not their food or their cool waterproof shell—because ideas are free.

12. Always leave an itinerary with a responsible party, then follow it. Make a conscious decision not to take risks. If you have a conflict in a group, retreat and then trust your instincts.

13. Go on the Internet and find a star/satellite chart for the area you will be visiting. These charts can tell you when you will see a satellite fly by and in what part of the sky to look. This is a great late-evening activity for the little ones.

14. Be the parent, not a wimp. If for some reason times are tough (rain, all your food stolen by a bear, mosquitoes eating you alive, tent just fell apart, kids crying, you were just hit by a meteor) be positive and supportive of your child. Deal with the situation and move on. They look to you for strength and fortitude, so fake it.

15. Tell bad puns and scary stories. You have a captive audience, and being the victim of a good eye-roll never hurt anyone.

16. Understand that dirt is OK, and it is part of the fun. Everyone will actually appreciate the ability to take a shower when they return.

17. Do your part to protect the areas you backpack in. When you return, contact local groups and agencies and see how you can help keep the wilderness such a special place.

18. When you put your bear canister away for the night, make sure to put it a good distance from your tent. Be sure, too, that the location you place it in will not allow the bear to give it a few good whacks and watch it fly off a cliff or into the middle of a lake. For entertainment, bears enjoy watching canisters fly.

19. If you are venturing into high-altitude terrain and you live at low elevation, try to spend a day or two acclimating to the altitude before starting your trip. Once the trip has begun, take it easy the first day of the hike.

20. Laugh, giggle, guffaw, whoop, titter, and chuckle as much as possible.

CHAPTER 5

A Three-Day Trip

When we go backpacking, I love it when we find a new lake
with islands and gigantic rocks. The rocks are always fun to
jump off of and make a big splash. I like playing cards and
hunting for flat rock tables to play on. Also chasing away
squirrels from our food bags, and going exploring in the
forest.

—Morgan Paulson, 15

People who have not yet backpacked with their child, or backpacked at all for that matter, might wonder what will really happen
on that first trip with a child. For your entertainment and enlight-
enment I present a hypothetical three-day trip.

The Night Before the Trip

The day is almost upon you. On the floor of your living room
is a big pile of stuff that looks too big to fit into a car, let alone
a backpack. Little Ralphie is excited and has his pack all ready to
go. He has a few little doohickies strapped to the outside of the
pack, and an illegal piece of candy that he hid in the bottom when
you were not looking. You are nervous, with the feeling that there

must be something you are forgetting. Finally, you go through the backpacking list (the one in this book, of course) one more time and believe you have everything. Then you begin the process of stuffing it all into the backpack. The first attempt leaves the pack filled to the brim and a big pile still sitting on the floor. You look at the list one more time and remove a few items to the chagrin and whining of Little Ralphie ("But Dad, what will I do out there without my toys?!"). Finally, you begin packing again. This time you put your sleeping bag at the bottom without a stuff sack and pack it down tight. Next up is the bear canister loaded with lots of food, which somehow fits sitting upright in the pack. Then you cram the tent to one side of the pack. Next come all the little soft items that get stuffed in all the nooks and crannies. Socks, shirt, pants, etc. . . . . Finally, near the top go the water filter, stove, and various other items that you may need quick access to. In the small top pocket you put lunch for the first day, the toiletries in a plastic bag, sunscreen, and a few snacks—the things you will need over and over again. Either inside, if there is room, or attached to the back if not, go your sleeping pad and a Camelback or other water hydration system. Whew, it's ready. It all got in there, and when you pick it up . . . Ah, when you pick it up. Well, if you could pick it up, it would weigh a lot. Finally, you get it up on your back somehow and realize when you step on a scale that it weighs 42 pounds. Not too bad, but it could be better. Welcome to backpacking with your children. You will spend the next 10 trips scratching your head trying to come up with a way to lower a little weight. Perhaps you should reread the rest of this book.

You tuck Little Ralphie into bed, answer all of his questions about the trip one more time and then say good-night. You get into bed and as you are about to nod off ask yourself: Did I put toothpaste in? What about an extra pair of socks? There is still time to go check everything once more before going to sleep.

Day One

The alarm goes off, and you feel refreshed and ready to hit the trail. You fix yourself your *last* civilized breakfast, brush your teeth with the electric toothbrush for the *last* time, use the toilet for the *last* time, and then coerce tired Little Ralphie into the car. You stop at your friend George's house, and Ralphie perks up at the arrival of his buddy Dylan. An hour later you are at the trailhead.

After a half-hour of organizing, taking several trips behind trees for bathroom breaks, and double- and triple-checking your bags, the four of you are ready. For the first ½ mile, the boys are practically running, laughing and joking, yelling, "Come on, Dad, let's go," and stopping to throw rocks. Then it comes, those immortal words, "When are we going to be there?" The first time you hear the words they are said with a cheery, elevated tone. Later it will digress to a pleading tone, before graduating to whining. Somehow, however, with the use of cajoling, threats, bribery, and a little bit of whining of your own, your group arrives at your camping spot: a spectacular mountain lake surrounded by high granite walls with scattered groves of fir trees. On the other side of the lake is a grassy, marshy area, with patches of aspen trees. The sky is a deep dark blue, and the sun is bright and warm.

When you arrive at the lake, the first thing you do is hurl your pack down and take the load off. After a few minutes of relaxation and making such profound comments as, "Whew" and "I feel light," the two adults wander around looking for the perfect campsite, while the kids lie there in a state of stupefaction for a few minutes before throwing rocks into the lake.

You find the perfect spot. It's on a little bluff, just a short walk from the lake, but far enough away to meet the 200 feet rule. There are several good tent sites with views and no widow makers (dead trees or suspended branches leaning over the tent site). About 75 feet away is a nice, flat piece of granite sheltered from the wind

Are we there yet?

that will be perfect as a kitchen. The whole area will catch a gentle breeze and is a good distance from a marshy or wet area, so the mosquitoes should be minimal. As you look further, you don't notice large piles of animal poop, so you are not camping right on top of a marmot or squirrel home. Finally, as you look down to the lake you can see a good-sized rock right at water's edge—the perfect place to filter water or go for a swim. This is it, your wonderful home for a few days.

Once your spot is selected, the first thing you do is drag Ralphie back from the lake and eat the sandwich you brought for lunch. Then it's time to set up the tent on the most level site, with the head of the tent at the highest point. The weather is pleasant, so you leave the rain fly off, but keep it handy for quick use if needed later. Once the tent is set up, you open up the valves on your sleeping pads so they start to fill with air, and then put your sleeping bags, the pads, clothing, and anything else you might need at night into the tent. You make sure you know where your headlamp is in case you need it in the middle of the night. Once the pad is halfway full of air, you finish blowing it up, and now you have a place to rest or nap if needed. You are pretty well set. Your pack is emptied out so you can get to kitchen supplies, and the tent won't blow away in the wind. Also, once the tent is up, you feel like this is your camping spot, and other backpackers will see that they need to find another spot, hopefully a good distance away. It is considered rude to camp too close to someone else in a wilderness area. I still remember a trip I made in a cold mid-October. I was near a beautiful mountain lake, there was not a soul in sight, and there were lots of great camping sites all around the lake. A woman comes up to me and says, "Are you camping here?" to which I say, "Ah, yes. . . ." "Oh, good," she says. "We will set up right over here" (about 100 feet away). Not exactly the privacy I wanted, but apparently the feeling of security she was looking for.

Before you can take a break and play you have one more camp duty—filtering water. Water filtering is actually quite relaxing. It gives you a few minutes to sit by the shore of a lake and gaze at the scenery as you quietly pump away. A bit of meditation a few times a day. Kids enjoy this task as well. After filling up all the bottles, you place them in the shade.

Now that your afternoon chores are complete, you are free to enjoy this warm and sunny day. You pull out the camera and sneak a few pictures of Ralphie and Dylan playing in the lake, then jump in yourself, after which you spend some time on a warm, smooth rock. Then you chat about nothing with Ralphie before he wanders off to explore a pile of rocks next to a strange-looking tree. You roll over onto your back and watch the clouds roll by, then just before you drift off to sleep, you roust yourself again for another dunking in the lake. This backpacking stuff is hard work, eh?

It is fascinating to watch the children at play. They need no toys as long as there are lots of rocks, frogs, and sticks around. Their imaginations are alive with ways to make something out of nothing. These are the kids that get bored in five minutes at home if they don't have a computer or a TV, but here they can spend hours with a pile of rocks and a couple of twigs. It is the innocent laughter that makes you smile. The hours roll by as you jot a few things in your journal and shoot the bull with Dylan's dad. You are practicing the art of nothingness.

Eventually, the kids get hungry, and it is time to think about dinner. You set up your kitchen, dig through the bear canister for a meal, get your bowls and utensils out, and boil the water. Soon, the four of you are sauntering over to the dining room rock and leisurely and quietly you eat while watching the gentle breeze softly cross the lake. A Clark's Nutcracker squawks and flies over-head, and a squirrel scampers under a small rock. In the distance, an eagle rides the thermals, spiraling in the deep blue. Finished with the main course, you delve deeper into the canister for more snacks and then use some of the remaining water from the stove to clean up your bowls and utensils, which are then left out on a rock to dry.

The sun is starting to get lower in the sky, but hours of light remain. Dylan breaks out a deck of cards, and he and Ralphie are soon chattering and playing, while you and George talk about life and how you would change it if you could. You talk about how nice it would be to be in the woods all the time and not have your life ruled by work and obligations. Then after a healthy sigh of realization, you join in the card game.

The wispy high clouds make for a blazing pink and orange sunset. As twilight approaches, a few bats begin to flit overhead and the evening chores begin. Teeth are brushed. Food is put away in the canister, which is then placed a few hundred feet away (close enough to hear the bear if you are awake, but not so close that he will wake you up). Everything you will need after dark is tossed into the tent, and extra clothing layers are slowly added as the temperature drops. You smile when you realize that you don't have to go home tonight, that in the morning you will wake up in this same, wonderful place, and you still won't have to go home tomorrow either. You then go back and drag the canister back, because you forgot to take your medicine and your toothpaste was in Ralphie's pocket. After warnings about bears mauling him in the middle of the night if there is any food left out of the bear canister, Ralphie finally sheepishly admits to the candy in his pack. As the sky gets darker, everyone pulls their sleeping pads out of the tent and lies down on a flat rock to look at the stars, watch the satellites go by, and tell scary stories. It is beyond me why we insist on telling scary stories to people when they are in places where they are most likely to be scared by them. Tradition. Finally, Ralphie asks if he can go to sleep, so you pile into the tent, and he falls fast asleep. Even though it is now quite cold outside, you are getting cozy in your sleeping bag when thoughts turn to having to go to the bathroom one more time. You wait, somehow deceiving yourself that the feeling will go away, and you really won't have to brave the freezing temperatures in the dark for the quick pee. Finally, you give up and find the release you seek and take one more cold look at the stars. You will never see as many stars as in the middle of the night on a backpacking trip (unless of course you don't have your glasses on, in which case you will see nothing).

Day Two

Mornings in your camp are very special times. There is nothing quite as peaceful as a cold morning in the wilderness. And it is a cold morning. A bit of frost sits on the backpack outside your tent. Ralphie is snoring next to you, but you have a powerful urge to find and water a tree, again. Without waking up the little rugrat,

Campers and cards go together.

you put on every stitch of clothing and gently exit from the tent. Afterward, you sit quietly and watch the hushed lake, perfectly still so that the mountain has a clear mirror image reflected in its surface. The morning birds slowly get more and more active, singing a chorus to the new day. You emerge from your daydream and boil some water for hot chocolate. The chocolate is slowly nursed, warming the hands and the heart. So quiet. Once finished, you silently walk around the area, clicking pictures and sitting on a rock and writing. Eventually, Ralphie emerges, and you boil more water for breakfast.

It is a layover day. You have nowhere you have to be. How often do you have a day that you have nowhere you have to be? This day is available to do nothing else but play. After breakfast it is off to the woods for the perfect spot for bathroom duties, and then you bombproof your campsite. Bombproofing means leaving your camp so that your gear could survive a hurricane. You put any gear that you are not taking with you in your tent and then make sure everything is held down securely. The next step is to store any smelly stuff in the bear canister, which is placed in a secure spot, preferably in the shade of a tree. With water and lunch in your pack, the four of you head off on a short walk to a nice viewpoint above the lake. The pace is leisurely, and on the way back the kids play in a creekbed, while you look at the trees and watch a chickadee. The afternoon is spent in the lake or on a rock next to it. Ralphie says you were snoring while he was swimming, but you don't remember. After another dip in the lake you talk to the boys about girls. All agree that they are a pain, but they have their pluses. You ask them about what they want to be when they grow up, and why when it comes to bellybuttons some people have innies, and others, outies. You know that day two of a back-packing trip is the best time you will ever find to talk to your children. They are more relaxed than the first day, and on the last day kids are already thinking about getting out and back to their own world.

The day slowly winds down, and the evening becomes a routine version of what you did the night before. It's another beautiful sunset and more pretty stars to see. Tonight, when it is time for bed, Ralphie is more rested, so you lie in the tent and read books with your headlamps. Just before falling asleep, Ralphie asks you, "Do you think Mom misses us?" Being a good parent, you lie, "I am sure she does."

Day Three

You wake up and tell yourself you don't want to leave and decide there really is no need to hurry. With hot cocoa in hand you watch and feel the sun slowly march from rock to rock as it rises above the horizon. The warmth soaks into your bones, and breakfast soon satisfies you. After breakfast you reluctantly begin to pack it up. Everything comes out of the tent, and then you lift the tent up and put it on its side to dry out the bottom. By the time the tent is dry, all of your stuff is organized and in a pile. It is warm now, and another swim is in order before hiking out. Another half-hour lying on a warm rock, and then you pack it up and begin hiking out. You chose a different route for the return trip to see more terrain. The kids are happy and walk along swiftly. You pass another lake, an excellent place for lunch and a last dip. Finally, when you reach the trailhead there is happiness that the long hike is done, but sadness that the trip is over.

Once you are home, both you and Ralphie create huge piles of dirty laundry and gear in the middle of the kitchen. Mom and Sister remind you to clean up all the mess when you are done. Ralphie is all excited and tells Mom and Sis all about the trip and how much fun he had. You check everything over carefully and make sure it is OK and dry, clean the dishes, and then repack it in the plastic backpacking bin where it is all ready to go for the next trip.

The Next Day

You begin planning your next trip. There are lots of exciting possibilities, and you can't wait for the next time you can hit the trail. Maybe next year we could go farther or higher and stay longer.

CHAPTER 6

The Madcap, Zany Misadventures with Sarah and Hannah

I love to listen to stories (and tell a few) around the campfire.
I loved watching the stars and then seeing a satellite fly by.

—Camille Joubert, 10

So far we have dealt with the basics of turning your kids into back-packers. Now that you have heard my advice and suggestions and heard all about a hypothetical trip, you are probably asking your-self, "Well, that is all well and good, but what is it *really* like?" It is wonderful, and frustrating and wonderful again. It is like life, only more so, and sometimes less so. It is a little like this. . . .

Summer

It was my nine-year-old Hannah's third year on a backpacking trip in 2002. While in previous years it was a bit like pulling teeth to get her to go, this year she was excited and perhaps more involved with the planning than I was. She wanted to organize the meals, go buy the stuff we needed, and seemed to be up on every little detail of the trip. Every night when I tucked her in bed, she would have some little comment like, "Can we bring lots of beef jerky this time?" or "How far do we have to hike again?" followed shortly after by, "Do we really have to hike that far?"

Only 15 more breaks, and we'll be there.

Our trip to Loch Leven Lakes in the northern Sierra was marvelous. The three delightful lakes are warm and shallow, and have tiny fairy-tale islands topped by miniature whitebark pines. Surrounding the lakes is a jumble of granite outcroppings waiting to be explored by kids. We spent the days wandering around in the rocks and admiring the views, fishing without ever catching anything, and swimming back and forth from island to shore. After swimming, we would shiver until the heat from the rocks had warmed us enough that we were ready for another dip. At night, we talked and talked and then lay in our sleeping bags and listened to a chorus of frogs, serenading us to sleep.

HOT AND HEAVY AT ROCK LAKE

Sarah at 12 was turning into a pleasant backpacking partner as well. With only a few complaints, she always went with the flow and had a great time. Our trip that year was to Rock Lake in the

Sierra Buttes area, a few hours north of Lake Tahoe. It was the hottest time of the year, and our well-named lake was completely surrounded by hot red rock with just a few scraggly trees that provided no shade. We baked. We wondered whether some sort of space-time vortex had transported us to the equator. It was so hot that we had to be in the water almost continuously during the day, and we broiled on top of our sleeping bags at night. The girls invented new games to play in the water and attempted to fish with a stick and a piece of line. (I am not a fisherman, but on many of my trips with the kids they have made several half-hearted attempts to catch fish, usually with a stick and line, or whatever they could dig out of their packs. Our total catch comes to a grand total of: Zero. That's OK, I am sure I would have been the one to have to deal with removing the fish from the hook and depositing them back where they belong.) I think it was just an excuse to be standing in the water holding a stick. Several times they came out screaming about a snake, but I never saw one. Which is a good thing, because I would have been screaming, too. In the end, they were troupers and kept their spirits up even after hiking up a dusty trail in 90-degree weather and then baking for a few days. On the way home we rewarded ourselves with one of the wonderful ways to end a backpacking trip—the guilt-free trip to the burger joint. Nothing quite like a few giant cheeseburgers in an air-conditioned dive to bring your spirits up. Once they had cooled off and a few French fries had reached their stomachs, they began talking about where they would like to go next year.

The Year of Lightning

We had two tremendous adventures in 2003. First, ten-year-old Hannah and I went to Lake Aloha in Desolation Wilderness. The views of the becalmed surface of Aloha with the Crystal Range reflected in its crystal waters were sublime. Hannah's fourth backpacking trip was a glorious few days, our best trip yet. We had great companions, stunning views, and plenty of options for adventure surrounding us. One afternoon, by wading and swimming from one little rocky island to the next, we slowly and joyfully worked our way halfway across the shimmering blue lake. Later, we journeyed to the other side of the lake and posed for funny pictures under downed trees and up against slimy rocks.

Of course, every backpack trip has its challenges and hurdles. Our first hurdle came around dinnertime of the first night. My friend Doug had volunteered to clean my stove and prepare it for the trip. I packed it in my bag, thinking (that is where the problem usually starts) that he would have the gas can and the little piece that connects the stove and the fuel bottle. He *had* the fuel bottle, he thought *I* had the little connecter piece. We looked at each other and did what camping buddies should do: Blamed it on ourselves and then quickly moved on to determine Plan B. The first part of Plan B was to eat tomorrow's lunch for dinner tonight. Then it was decided that first thing in the morning Doug would hike out the five miles to the trailhead with just some water and a day pack, drive to South Lake Tahoe, and borrow a stove from a friend. By 1 PM the next day, we were worry-free for the rest of the trip. Or so we thought (cue the eerie-scary music playing in the background).

For the next two days, we were treated to spectacular sunrises and sunsets as wispy clouds made for picture-perfect skies. It was an idyllic life, what backpacking can be all about. Swimming in pools sheltered from the wind, lying on warm rocks watching clouds roll by, playing cards, doing absolutely nothing in an absolutely beautiful spot. Evening strolls along the lakeshore. Ducking into snow caves that dripped water on our heads from the last remaining snowfields. Standing on top of snowfields suspended on the edge of the lake. We even enjoyed the most time-honored of childhood camping experiences—the funny skit. The girls spent

Who says you can't walk on water?

hours secretly planning their elaborate production. The full presentation lasted about 10 minutes and we dads were just scratching our heads trying to figure out what that was all about. But they
had fun and that's what's important.

As we began our walk out to the trailhead on the third day, the
clouds in the distance became ominous. By the time we were halfway back we could hear thunder and see bright flashes of lightning.
The storm was approaching rapidly, getting closer and closer every
minute. Doug, the weather fanatic, kept gauging our distance from
the lightning and had hopes that we could make it to the trailhead
before we got caught in the storm (or at least that is what he told
us, perhaps he already knew we were dead meat and didn't want
to scare the kids). Finally, about a mile before we reached the ferry
dock, the raucous barrage was right over our heads. Bolts of lightning were shooting out of the sky, and the roaring crack of thun-

der seemed to be continuous. As the lightning strikes got closer and closer, Hannah emitted little high-pitched squeaky noises with each blast and began walking much faster than I had ever seen her walk before. Then the sky opened up, and the rain and hail started to come down in buckets. Doug quickly built a shelter with a rain fly and hiking poles, and we huddled shivering underneath it in a grove of trees. It was just in the nick of time, as the next 15 minutes was a constant deluge. The little gully we were crouched in (that's funny; it didn't look like a gully when we dove in there) quickly became a raging stream, and our backpacks, which we somehow inadvertently left out of the shelter, were now wringing wet and soaking up water like sponges. The storm eventually passed, and we then confronted the Herculean effort of lifting those soaking wet backpacks onto our backs. Fortunately, it was the end of the trip, all the food was gone, and it was not far to the dock. It was a glorious sight to see the little ferryboat chugging out of the mist at Upper Echo Lake. As we started across the lake, we could see towering flames and smoke rising from a huge pine tree high up on a granite buttress above. The grim-faced boat passengers quietly pointed to the fire, and I looked past the soaking wet brown curls covering my daughter's face to see a flash of recognition light her eyes. Loud booms, smoking tree: lightning bad. She was happy to be out of the woods and ready to go home, but still talks joyfully about the rest of the trip. "Can we go somewhere next year where they don't have lightning?" If only it were possible.

NOT JUST LIGHTNING, BUT LOTS OF RAIN, TOO

Hannah's trip that year was a piece of cake compared to my trip with her older sister, Sarah. We didn't mess around with a few beautiful sunny days to lull us into submission; we started right out from the trailhead under threat of rain, the clouds thickening up as we walked. We had just made it to the camping spot at Fontanillis Lake in Desolation Wilderness and quickly threw up our tents before the rain started to come down. At first, Sarah and I felt all warm and snug in our tent, listening to the rain and hail pounding on the rocks and the tent. Sure, the lightning seemed a little too close for comfort, and the rain was really coming down hard, but I was sure the tent would keep us warm and dry. Then we looked out the tent window and noticed that our hastily selected, supposedly fantastic tent spot was actually at the bottom of a gully and the tent was starting to float in several inches of water. As long as the interior of the tent stayed dry it seemed quite comfortable, so we floated along on our water bed waiting for the rains to stop. As soon as it cleared up, we emerged from the tent to start shovel duty. Frantically working away with our pooper scoopers, we dug two trenches to remove the water from around the tent. After an hour of shoveling, the water slowly receded, and we were able to pick up the tent and set it on the rocks to dry. In between shoveling, we were running around placing all the other wet objects on rocks and in trees in a valiant effort to dry everything.

Sarah and I spent a pleasant evening in our now dried-out tent, with stars peeping through the breaks in the clouds above our heads, but way off in the distance I could see lightning strikes bouncing off the clouds. We awoke the following morning to partly cloudy skies. Taking advantage of what we knew might be a brief respite, we climbed up rocky knobs to enjoy the view, walked down alongside the spectacular cascade that falls between Fontanillis Lake and Upper Velma Lake, and enjoyed the beauty of this desolate paradise to its fullest. We knew that as the clouds slowly got thicker, we were like condemned prisoners doing our best to enjoy life now before it was time for the gallows.

By mid-afternoon it again started to rain. It was not the quick-downpour-and-now-it's-over rain of the day before; this was more of a slow, nonstop water torture. It was a steady, drizzling rain that kept us in our tents for hour upon hour. We emerged briefly for

The rain won't keep me from smiling when I'm
with my friend at Fontanillis Lake.

a quick wet meal in the soft rain, and then it was back in the tent
again. Was that Noah that just rowed past?

Spending hours in a little backpack tent with nothing to do
can be a bit boring. How boring? Sarah and I actually took turns
reading aloud the first aid instruction book. She learned about lac-
erations, sprains and strains, and abrasions. I skipped the section
on gynecological problems. It rained all night long, but we stayed
dry in our bags. I discovered the challenges of peeing in the rain in
the middle of the night. It is not as much the standing in the drizzle
that gets you wet, as the attempt to crawl underneath the wet rain
fly on your way in and out.

In the morning, with the sun making another brief appear-
ance, we writhed once again out of our wet tents. After 14 hours
of separation, Sarah was happy to get reacquainted with her friend

Morgan. It doesn't matter if your tents are 20 feet apart, if it is raining like crazy, you are no longer on the same trip. We had been cocooned in our own little world that got smaller and smaller every minute. After brief greetings, we looked up at the next wave of clouds rolling in and decided it was time to pack it up and get the heck out of there. We hiked fast and made it back to the car in record time, happy in our dryness. As we drove away from the trailhead, the rain started splattering down again on the windshield.

Where Are You, My Hiking Friend? And, Oh, Yeah . . . More Rain

By 2004, the girls were getting bigger and stronger. They were capable of taking longer and more difficult trips, and getting ready to take a trip was a breeze. Hannah at 11 was ready to roll into a new adventure—a more difficult hike to a lake that was not on a trail. The Bayview Trail into Desolation Wilderness wastes no time, starting out very steep for the first mile up to a viewpoint above Emerald Bay. Hannah's friend Maiya wasn't with us, but instead was going to walk in later with her dad. Difficult adventures are a little easier with a friend around to egg you on, so Hannah was bummed not to have her friend with her to share in the suffering. With a friend around, kids tend to keep their whining to a minimum. They have no such compunction when it comes to Dad; just let the whining rip.

From the Emerald Bay viewpoint, we slowly made our way farther uphill to a lunch spot and a swim at Granite Lake. From here it was an even longer jaunt up the cleavage between the teo Maggies Peaks to the saddle. Then the worst was over as a tired Hannah and I journeyed mostly downhill toward the Velma Lakes. In the middle of the afternoon we heard a few cracks of thunder with lightning in the distance, but it didn't seem very threatening. Eventually we headed off-trail and followed the creek down to trailless Lower Velma Lake. It is a glorious adventure for a kid to travel off-trail, to look at a map and follow the drainage instead of a trail. And Lower Velma is a gorgeous lake surrounded by high granite cliffs. We knew that Doug and Maiya would be there shortly, but we decided to go ahead and set up camp. As we were surveying for the best site, it began to softly rain. Feeling like it might begin to rain harder, we found a lower spot in a clump of trees, whipped out the rain fly, and watched as the rain started coming down hard with lightning in the distance. Fortunately, it only lasted a half-hour, after which we emerged from our cocoon to a beautiful sight—deep blue sky and sunshine, with a few drops of rain seeming to slowly float down from the clear sky. The drops must have left the clouds before they rolled on past. The air was crystal clear and crisp, and we quickly located a wonderful campsite on a bluff above the lake. It had spectacular views of the entire lake and plenty of room for tents and cooking. We filtered water, set up the tent, and waited in anticipation of the arrival of our buddies. And waited. And waited. At 6 PM we were getting worried and wondered where they could be. Finally, we decided to eat without them, but our plans for dinner were thwarted by a stove that we could not get to work. Hannah reminded me that out of her five backpacking trips she had only eaten stove-cooked food on one, and that had required Doug to make a ten-mile roundtrip hike to get a stove that worked. (Geez, Hannah, you're bad luck, why am I hiking with you?) In my defense, three of those trips had just been for one night so we did not bring in a stove and went with cold food. On another of the trips, we could not get the stove working and so we cooked on a fire. Perhaps I am not very good at operating a stove. Now you know why I was so excited about recently acquiring a JetBoil stove. Even I can operate it.

We decided it wasn't a problem, because our friends would be there soon and they had an extra stove. At 7 PM we walked up to higher ground in an attempt to get cell phone reception to figure out where in the world they might be. At 8 PM it was getting dark, so in between swatting the 5 billion mosquitoes, we put together salami and cheese for dinner and readied for bed. Hannah was sad, worried, perplexed, and disappointed. Mostly my analytical little girl was confused; it just didn't make sense that they would not have arrived yet. At 9 PM, we were all warm and cozy and gazing up at the stars, but Hannah was tearfully proclaiming that she wanted to go home. While I was firm that we were not getting up now in the dark and hiking out, I did try to allay her fears and let her know that there must be an explanation. I kept it to myself that I was quite worried as well.

In the morning we awoke to a beautiful dawn. My back was a bit stiff from the Thermarest pad, which had sprung a leak in the middle of the night, and I was a bit tired from attempting to blow up the pad twice, but it was a new day. Perhaps today our missing explorers would pop up. I fixed cereal for breakfast and we waited. And waited. After the 3,000th "They should have been here by now," the two worrywarts decided it was time to try another cell phone call, so we walked once again up toward Middle Velma Lake. And what to our wondering eyes should appear, but Doug and Maiya, too, strolling down the hill. Yippee!!

Instantly the trip changed. Our gloom and doom was spirited away on a gentle breeze. A very happy Hannah ran off to play with her friend and make up for lost time. Swimming in the lake, playing in the stream, laughing, and running. Once again she could be a happy kid in camp. A great little creek dumped into Lower Velma Lake just below our campsite. It had deep pools for swimming and short slimy sections that you could slide down. Even a docile black snake sunning himself on the rocks couldn't dampen their excitement. While watching the kids play, I found out the story from Doug. They had left later than planned and ended up getting caught right in the middle of the worst part of the thunderstorm at Granite Lake. They quickly set up camp and watched it rain for

Another day in paradise at Paradise Lake.

several hours and decided to spend the night there. This was all a very logical explanation, but in the darkness of a lonely camp it is easy to think the worst.

The rest of our trip was glorious. Swimming, picture-taking, more swimming, laughing, walking, exploring. When out in the wilderness, you will find moments of absolute bliss, mixed with moments of fear and frustration. The trick is to get through the tough spots and revel in the glory of the special times.

RAIN AND TENT-PITCHING SCHOOL

My trip with Sarah that year was like most of the rest of our trips: Rain, plus quite a bit of hail and lightning, but I jump ahead. I decided that the 13-year-old girls were ready for a longer trip at higher elevation, so we set out to Star Lake on the Tahoe Rim Trail.

Situated right below Freel Peak and Jobs Sister, two of the highest peaks in the Lake Tahoe area, Star Lake has a wonderful feeling of remoteness, while still being relatively easy to hike to. It's a little piece of heaven in the dry Carson Range east of Lake Tahoe. The hike to the lake was beautiful, and it was a sunny day. We passed the saddle near Freel Peak and headed past gnarly whitebark pines on a gentle downhill to Star Lake. Once past the Freel saddle the thunder bumpers began popping up and the sounds of thunder could be heard nearby. There does seem to be a theme with these stories. Like I said in the beginning of the book, it really doesn't rain every day in the Sierra, only on the days I am backpacking. When we reached the lake it started to rain lightly, and we determined we'd better set up camp. Then it started to hail. Hard. From the time the hail started until our tent was set up was less than two minutes. Oh, yeah, Sarah and I are an awesome tent-setting-up machine—as long as it is hailing like crazy. Once it was up, we plunged in and listened to the roar of the hail. Within minutes, surrounded by several inches of hail, the tent became ice cold, and we had to climb inside our sleeping bags. The water in my Camelback, which was resting on the floor, had gone from warm to bitterly cold. Our past rainy experiences had trained us well as we happily read books and played cards for an hour while the hail and rain poured down. Ultimately, it stopped (which reminds me of the farmer who, when asked during a long rainstorm, "will this rain ever stop?" replied, "always has"). We climbed out of our tent to behold a cloud of soft steam gently rising from Star Lake. Jobs Sister was partially obscured in the clouds high above, and we breathed in the sweet smell of wet pine trees. It was truly spectacular. As I have said before, when you are camping, all bad things are followed by good things, and vice versa.

The rest of our trip was uneventful, which was just fine. On a bright, sunny day we wandered past a blindingly white mountain of quartz, to a rock outcropping and a dip in the very cold waters of Star Lake. We journeyed up a small creek to a lush meadow, with a few acres of mossy green amidst the brown sand of the slopes of Freel Peak. Card games went on for hours, interrupted occasionally by the search for the next perfect flat piece of granite to play on. And the girls enjoyed senseless wanderings and newly invented games in the rocks. When you backpack, in many ways whether you are 46 years old or 13 years old, you get to be 8. Enjoy it while you can.

CHAPTER 7

Conclusions

You only need one set of clothes for two weeks and you can
spend a whole day lying on a beach and that's a full day.
—Logan Greenwood, 15

Last-Minute Reminders

Wait, we're not quite done yet. . . . A few final things to remember:

1. Double-check everything twice to make sure you are not
   forgetting anything. And then check it all over one more
   time, especially if you are over 40! Wait, go back into the
   house one more time, your sunglasses are still on the
   kitchen table, and you left your medicine on the coun-
   ter. You'd better double-check that the kitchen stove is
   turned off, because you know you will worry about it
   otherwise.

2. Make sure your equipment works and is in good repair
   before you leave on the trip. This is especially important
   for the stove, tent, headlamp, hiking boots, water filter,
   sleeping pad, and sleeping bag. Not only should it be in
   good working order, you should also be sure you know
   how to use it. Do you know how to set up that fancy

It doesn't get much better than this.

new tent you just bought? You could do what I did the first few trips with a new tent, bring along a picture of it set up. Then you can say, "Oh, yeah, the black pole goes OVER the red poles!" How about the stove? Have you cooked with it ahead of time to make sure it works so that you will be eating hot food? Does the water filter have some sort of green organisms growing out of the bottom of it, or is it nice and clean and ready to go? Are the batteries in your headlamp and camera charged? Does the sleeping pad have a hole in it? Are your boots in good shape, with laces that will last through the trip?

3. When you lock your car at the trailhead, make sure your keys are not in the car. It is the little things in life that can pop up and wreck your whole day, or week. Be sure to remove valuables from your car (best to leave them at home) and any food that might attract critters. Bears, marmots, raccoons, and other wild animals look at a car as just the packaging that needs to be removed before getting to the good stuff inside. Make sure there is no good stuff inside. There is a bear sitting behind that big tree waiting for you to leave so he can open up his lunch box (your car). In fact, I have heard reports of bears at Yosemite waiting for tourists to get out of the car, and while the doors are still open coming out of the trees on two legs. Then while the tourists scream and run away in panic, the bears help themselves to the goodies in the car. Nice of those people to leave the doors open for the bears.

4. Tell someone where you will be going and when you will be back. Be sure that they allot a little extra time so that someone isn't initiating a search for you while you are obliviously gazing at a meadow full of flowers, forgetting about the time. Relax and enjoy the trip and don't worry about time, until the last day.

A Final Note

It is not necessary to read 1,000-page books on all of the intricacies of backpacking to pick up your kids and hit the trail. All you need to do is review the basics, make sure you have everything you need, plan the right trip for their abilities, and go do it. Start out with an easy, shorter trip and work your way up to a longer trip. Make it fun and have some fun, and who knows, someday you could be spending several weeks with your child hiking the Tahoe Rim Trail or the John Muir Trail. Whatever you do, try backpacking with your children. If you are looking for a special experience with your child, and a way to reacquaint yourself with nature, this is the way to do it.

Things to Read

Reference Works

Aside from a good first aid book and a field guide to animals and plants for your favorite area, I recommend the following basic primers:

Arno, Stephen F. *Discovering Sierra Trees.* Yosemite Association, 1973.

If you run across this hard-to-find, inexpensive little gem of a book be sure to pick it up. The black-and-white drawings of Sierra trees are awe-inspiring and capture the trees better than any photos I have seen. It has everything you need to know about trees in the Sierra and in a quick and easy-to-understand format.

Backhurst, Paul, ed. *Backpacking California.* Berkeley, Calif.: Wilderness Press, 2001.

A hefty summary of dozens of great backpacking routes in California. One of the first places I look when planning my next backpacking trip in the Sierra Nevada.

Blackwell, Laird R. *Wildflowers of the Sierra Nevada and the Central Valley.* Vancouver, Canada: Lone Pine Publishing, 1999.

Check out this or one of Laird's other wildflower books for flower identification in the Sierra. They all have wonderful photos that make it easy to identify the plants.

Fletcher, Colin, and Chip Rawlins. *The Complete Walker IV.* New York: Alfred A. Knopf, 2002.

This humongous book has everything you could ever possibly need to know about hiking, and the writing is quite witty and fun, although a bit long for most readers.

Hauserman, Tim. *The Tahoe Rim Trail: A Complete Guide for Hikers, Mountain Bikers, and Equestrians.* Berkeley, Calif.: Wilderness Press, 2002.

If you are interested in hiking or camping on the 165-mile Tahoe Rim Trail this is the book for you, and although his kids would probably beg to differ, I heard the author is really cool.

Meyer, Kathleen. *How to Shit in the Woods.* Berkeley, Calif.: Ten Speed Press, 1989.

More than you would ever want to know about the subject of poo. This book has reportedly sold over 2 million copies, which illustrates the power of a book title.

Morey, Kathy, and Mike White. *Sierra North.* 9th edition. Berkeley, Calif.: Wilderness Press, 2005.

Along with *Sierra South* this book should give you the information you need to hike anywhere in the Sierra Nevada range.

O'Bannon, Allen, and Mike Clelland. *Allen and Mike's Really Cool Backpackin' Book.* Helena, Mont.: Falcon Press, 2001.

A wonderful little lighthearted primer on backpacking. The section on how to use a topographic map is especially good. Clelland's drawings are very entertaining and look like they came right out of *Mad* magazine.

Schaffer, Jeffrey B. *The Tahoe Sierra.* Berkeley, Calif.: Wilderness Press, 1998.

Schaffer describes over 100 trails in the Lake Tahoe region. This book has been around since 1975 and is now on its fourth edition. It is an excellent resource that I refer to frequently.

Schlimmer, E. *Thru-Hikers Guide to America: 25 Incredible Trails You Can Hike in One to Eight Weeks.* Camden, Maine: Ragged Mountain Press, 2005.

You may never have heard of some of these trails, but after reading about them you may be enchanted enough to plan a visit. Schlimmer has a unique viewpoint on all things outdoors, and his book is a fun read.

White, Mike. *Top Trails—Lake Tahoe.* Berkeley, Calif.: Wilderness Press, 2004.

Winner of a Benjamin Franklin Outdoor Book Award. Rivals *The Tahoe Sierra* as a hiking source for the Tahoe Sierra region.

White, Mike. *50 Classic Hikes in Nevada.* Reno: University of Nevada Press, 2006.

A nice description of Mike's choices for the 50 best places to hike in Nevada. He uncovers some wonderful hidden gems.

Winnett, Thomas, and Melanie Findling. *Backpacking Basics.* 4th edition. Berkeley, Calif.: Wilderness Press, 1994.

A classic that has been around in various editions since 1972. Perhaps a bit outdated, but short and sweet and covers most of the basics.

Winnett, Thomas, Jason Winnett, Kathy Morey, and Lyn Haber. *Sierra South*. 7th edition. Berkeley, Calif.: Wilderness Press, 2001.

Combines with *Sierra North* to describe the best hikes in the Sierra Nevada.

Good Books to Read on the Trail

It is a good idea to bring along a lightweight, soft-cover book that will be entertaining to read via headlamp while waiting for the stars to appear, or alongside a mountain stream with the babble of running water next to you. A good little book can also be a sanity-saver when the rain comes down, and you have to spend hours in the tent. I look for a good read, perhaps with a few laughs, a well-turned story, a beautiful sentence. The best books always make me say, "Gee, I wish I could write like that."

Abbey, Edward. *Desert Solitaire: A Season in the Wilderness*. New York: Ballantine Books, 1998.

Abbey's poetic passion for the environment is a joy to read.

Alcorn, Susan. *We're in the Mountains, Not over the Hill— Tales and Tips from Seasoned Women Backpackers*. Oakland, Calif.: Shepherd Canyon Books, 2003.

To get a different perspective on backpacking, listen to the powerful voices of mature women backpackers, many in their sixties and seventies.

Bryson, Bill. *A Walk in the Woods*. New York: Random House, 1998.

This book about two totally unprepared and inept hikers' half-hearted attempt to hike the Appalachian Trail is one of the funniest books I have ever read. If you are going to go on a hike you have to read this book, if only to feel that at least you are more competent than these guys. If you are less competent then the bumbling Katz you probably shouldn't be out on the trail.

Callahan, Steven. *Adrift: Seventy-Six Days Lost at Sea*. New York: Ballantine Books, 1986.

Callahan's small sailboat sank just six days into a trip across the Atlantic Ocean. He spent the next two months floating in a life raft, clinging to life, before eventually landing in the Caribbean. Read this on a tough backpack trip to remind yourself that you are not really roughing it.

Doig, Ivan. *Dancing at the Rascal Fair*. New York: Harper-Collins, 1987.

Doig beautifully depicts the rustic life of the first homesteaders in western Montana. Doig's book *English Creek* continues the saga of this wonderful mythic place.

Duncan, David James. *The River Why*. New York: Bantam Books, 1984.

One of the best books ever written on living, loving, and nature. And pretty funny to boot. It may even make you want to go fishing.

Kingsolver, Barbara. *Prodigal Summer*. New York: Harper-Collins, 2000.

A beautiful story about the power and majesty of nature, and how humans fit into the picture.

Krakauer, Jon. *Into the Wild*. New York: Anchor Books, 1996.

The true story of a young man who was discovered dead in a remote part of Alaska. Krakauer investigates the man's life to discover how it led to this tragic end. It is an interesting story about the human quest for danger and expanding the envelope.

Lang, Susan. *Small Rocks Rising.* Reno: University of Nevada Press, 2002.

The intriguing story of an independent woman living all alone on a California homestead in the 1920s.

Leopold, Aldo. *A Sand County Almanac.* New York: Oxford University Press, 1949.

In this classic book, Leopold presents his concept of a land ethic in which he maintains that nature has intrinsic as well as financial value to humanity. His ideas were the basis of much of modern thought toward nature and its preservation.

McIntyre, Mike. *The Kindness of Strangers—Penniless Across America.* New York: Berkley Publishing, 1996.

This is the story of a man who starts out with no money in his pocket and through the kindness of strangers travels across America. I went to high school with the author and could visualize his big smile opening doors and hearts in his attempt to make it across the country.

Morgan, Marlo. *Mutant Message Down Under.* New York: Harper-Collins, 1991.

A white woman from America joins a group of Aborigines on a nomadic four-month journey around the Australian outback. If *Adrift* didn't do enough to put your petty difficulties in perspective, this book will certainly finish the job. Once you are finished reading, you will understand that a weekend backpacking with children is a piece of cake compared to living in the Australian desert for months eating bugs.

Muir, John. *My First Summer in the Sierra*. San Francisco: Sierra Club Books, 1988.

Muir's excitement with nature helped start the environmental movement. You do not really understand the power and glory of a tree until you hear Muir's description of one. This small book is an easy one to take along on a trip, but don't forget to read some of the other Muir classics.

Rand, Ayn. *The Fountainhead*. New York: Bobbs-Merrill Company, 1943.

Whether you agree with Ayn Rand's philosophy of independence and self-sufficiency or not, she will make you think.

Robbins, Tom. *Even Cowgirls Get the Blues*. New York: Bantam Books, 1976.

A relaxing and fun read by one of America's great writers. Once you have finished this one, start reading the rest of Robbins' novels.

Stegner, Wallace. *Where the Bluebird Sings to the Lemonade Springs*. New York: Modern Library, 2002.

A series of short stories and essays on life in the western United States by one of the region's greatest writers. *Angle of Repose* and *Crossing to Safety* are two very worthwhile Stegner novels, but read them before you hit the trail, because they are a bit heavy for the backpack.

Steinbeck, John. *The Grapes of Wrath*. New York: The Heritage Press, 1940.

This classic American writer's books all touch on nature and humanity. Aside from *The Grapes of Wrath,* I recommend: *Of Mice and Men, Travels with Charley,* and *In Dubious Battle.*

> Thoreau, Henry David. *Walden: Or, Life in the Woods.* Mineola, New York: Dover Publications, 1995.

In my mind Thoreau joins John Muir and Aldo Leopold as the grandfathers of nature literature.

> Wren, Christopher S. *Walking to Vermont: From Times Square into the Green Mountains.* New York: Simon and Schuster, 2004.

Wren was a foreign correspondent for the *New York Times.* When he retired he walked from his office in Manhattan to his new home in northern Vermont. A wonderful story about hiking and meeting people that is written with humor and humility.

Sara's Choices

My friend Sara Holm read my manuscript and came up with a great list of books also worth reading:

> Bass, Rick. *Winter, Notes from Montana.* Boston, Mass.: Houghton Mifflin. 1991.

> Brown, Chip. *Good Morning Midnight, Life and Death in the Wild.* New York: Riverhead Books, 2003.

> Carter, Forrest. *The Education of Little Tree.* Albuquerque: University of New Mexico Press, 1986.

> Lopez, Barry. *Crossing Open Ground.* New York: Vintage Books, 1989.

> MacLean, Norman. *A River Runs Through It.* Thorndike, Maine: G. K. Hall, 1993.

Ralston, Aron. *Between a Rock and a Hard Place*. New York: Atria Books, 2004.

Rawlins, C. L. *Sky Witness: A Year in the Wind River Range*. New York: Holt, 1993.

Williams, Terry Tempest. *Refuge: An Unnatural History of Family and Place*. New York: Vintage Books, 2001.

ACKNOWLEDGMENTS

For me, writing a book is a group effort. Aside from the people who hike with me, I try to get lots of friends to read it as the manuscript progresses. This allows me to get the honest scoop on how I am doing.

I have five friends who took the time to read through the whole manuscript and give me lots of helpful suggestions: Sara Holm, Cherie Turner, Daniella Hirschfield, Shannon Raborn, and Anne Greenwood. Thank you all; I could not have done it without you. A special kudos to Shannon for coming up with the title, *Monsters in the Woods*.

I received lots of other tips, suggestions, photos, and information from Karen Honeywell (infants and toddlers), Mary and John Carnell (food and gear), Patti Rudge, Mary Chambers, Dirk and Marti Schoonmaker, Jim and Jenny Backhus, Joe Pace, Denese and John Pillsbury, Katie and Jon Jubert, Mike White, and the staff at the Tahoe Rim Trail Association.

A special thanks goes to those children and parents who went on trips with me and taught me way more than I could have taught them. Morgan and Dave Paulson, Carly and Joe Leininger, Kelly and Jeff Holman, and Maiya, Logan, Anne, and Doug Greenwood.

To the folks at University of Nevada Press, thanks for turning my ideas into reality. Getting a book published does seem to take forever, but once the press whipped into high gear I was very impressed. Special thanks to Margaret Dalrymple, Sara Vélez Mallea, and Vicki Davies. I really enjoyed working with my editor, Ben Greensfelder, who made the editing process a breeze. When he said he laughed out loud reading the book, I think he meant it as a

compliment. If you are going to write about children it is important to think like a child.

Finally, my biggest thanks go to Sarah and Hannah. Thanks
for hiking with me, not whining too much, and being good kids
most of the time.

plant identification, 18
Plumas-Eureka State Park, 11
poison oak and ivy, 76; Ivy Block, for
 reaction prevention, 76
pooping, 86–87
preparation: reminders, 117–19; for
 trips, 17–20, 66; for health of
 backpackers, 80
Promoting Environmental Awareness
 in Kids. *See* PEAK

Q
quiet, 83–84

R
rainy weather, 57; dogs in, 64; on
 Fontanillis Lake trip, 108–11;
 infants and toddlers in, 53; on
 Lake Aloha trip, 107–8; on Star
 Lake trip, 115; in trees during,
 75; on Velma Lakes trip, 111–14.
 See also lightning
reasons, for backpacking with
 children, 1–5, 8–16
regulations, 82–88
Rock Lake, 11, 105
Round Top (mountain), 13
rules and regulations, 82–88

S
safety, 72–80: bears and, 66–70; dogs
 and, 62–64; fears, overcoming,
 64–66; first aid issues, 70–72;
 Leave No Trace, principles of,
 88; rules and regulations for,
 82–88; tips for, 72–73, 89, 90, 91,
 92, 119; water treatments for,
 80–82

Schlimmer, E., 16
shells, waterproof. *See* clothing
shirts. *See* clothing
shoes. *See* clothing
shorts. *See* clothing
Sierra Nevada, 77–78
sleeping bags, 27–28, 51–52
sleeping pads, 28–29
smoking, 85
snow: enjoying, 57; melting, 59–60;
 safety and, 77–78
socks. *See* clothing
sprains, avoidance of, 71
star-gazing, 56–57, 91
Star Lake, 12–13, 114–16
stoves, 29: JetBoil, 29, 112; in ultralight
 backpacking, 24
streams, 55–56, 76–77
sunburn, avoidance of, 71
sunstroke, avoidance of, 70
Superior Hiking Trail, 16
swimming, 76

T
Tahoe Rim Trail: description of, 15; as
 hiking destination, 11–12; Mary
 Chambers hiking, 7–8; Star Lake
 on, 12–13, 114–16; talus on,
 78–79
tents: as essential to bring, 29–31; in
 lightweight backpacking, 22;
 pitching in rain, 114–16; safety
 of, 75; setting up, 4; size of, 5; in
 ultralight backpacking, 23–24
three-day trip: day after trip, 102;
 first day of, 95–99; night before,
 93–94; second day of, 99–101;
 third day of, 101–2

Thru Hiker's Guide to America
(Schlimmer), 16
ticks, 75
toddlers. *See* infants and toddlers
toiletries, 22, 37
topographic maps. *See* maps
Trader Joe's, 39
trips, 103–5, 105–11, 111–16;
informing others of plans
for, 119; preparing for, 17–20;
termination of, 102. *See also*
three-day trip